THIS IS
CHILD HEALTH
IN THE HOME

Åke Gyllenswärd and Ulla-Britt Hägglund

THIS IS
CHILD HEALTH
IN THE HOME

A Practical Guide for Parents

Translated by DAVID LOUCH

Foreword by
Dr. DAVID HARVEY FRCP
Consultant Paediatrician
Queen Charlotte's Maternity Hospital, London

Harrap London

Foreword

There are many baby books available on the market, but it is more difficult for parents to find a book which gives clear advice about the many minor illnesses which happen during childhood. I was very pleased to see this book because we all admire the high standard of paediatric care in Sweden. The advice given by the authors is just as useful for British families and it was a good idea to translate it into English. All the problems that affect young children are well described and I am sure that this will be a book for families to keep at hand for easy reference. I think that the descriptions of the common infectious illnesses are particularly important, because children become feverish very frequently. It is important for you to have a clear idea of simple treatment so that your family doctor is not called too often. You should turn to him, however, whenever you are seriously worried about your child.

I like the information about what will happen when a child goes to hospital. If your child is admitted to hospital, please try and stay with him if you can.

David Harvey
London, June 1982

First published in Great Britain 1982
by HARRAP LIMITED
19–23 Ludgate Hill, London EC4M 7PD

First published by Bonnier Fakta Bokförlag AB,
Stockholm under the title Barnsjukdomar och Barnolycksfall

© *Bonnier Facta Bokförlag AB* 1981
English Translation © *Harrap Limited* 1982

ISBN 0 245-53914-X

Printed in Sweden

Preface

What we have aimed to do is to produce an easy-to-read, practical and profusely illustrated book on the diseases, injuries and health-care of children. The emphasis is on the sort of useful advice that will make it easier for parents to treat their children for minor complaints and domestic accidents. We have also attempted to advise parents on when and how to call in professional help, but we have purposely avoided discussing serious and chronic diseases requiring specialized treatment and regular contact with the doctor. Baby care is another area that receives scant attention, since most parents take their infants to clinics. Besides, many good books on this subject are already available.

The number of children injured in accidents is horrifyingly large. In this book we have done no more than outline the steps which can be taken to prevent such accidents. However, we hope that we have done something to encourage parents and others who work with children to take more pains to recognize potentially dangerous situations.

Admittedly, the material in a book such as this must be limited, but it has to be remembered that the situation in the field of public health has changed quite quickly in this country. Some illnesses have almost disappeared, while others have gained ground. Our resources for overcoming disease have been increased. In the past twenty years smallpox has been virtually eradicated all over the world. Diphtheria is now relatively rare, and so is polio. Congenital syphilis, which had such serious consequences, has virtually disappeared in this country, and tuberculosis has been repelled and is now a rare disease. Very few of our children suffer from vitamin deficiencies or a lack of iron. The fact that serious acute diarrhoea is now seldom seen in babies is mainly due to the good work of the welfare services. Nevertheless, if this satisfactory state of affairs is to be maintained, constant attention has to be paid to inoculation programmes, medical examinations and the dissemination of information on hygiene and balanced feeding.

On the other hand, we are being challenged by other diseases, diseases of which we were formerly ignorant or from which children died because medical knowledge was deficient and successful treatments had not been developed. Cystic fibrosis of the pancreas and other congenital infirmities – such as certain metabolic disturbances which can be controlled by special diets – are cases in point. Serious congenital malformations can be repaired by timely operations. Nevertheless, spina bifida (for example) can be accompanied by important functional disturbances demanding intensive medical and socio-medical care. Diabetes appears to be on the increase, as do allergies; although our means of treating these diseases have improved.

As these changes take place doctors find themselves having more to do with everyday illnesses which people used to treat themselves. Without doubt, most of the obviously needless visits to the doctor (often at inconvenient times) are not deliberate abuses but spring from uncertainty, anxiety and lack of knowledge. The modern family with small children is not always blessed with older, experienced relatives living close at hand and ready with sound advice. We hope that this book will take their place.

The authors

Contents

When should the doctor be consulted?

Parents soon learn how their children react, and have no problem in recognizing when something is wrong. However, it is not always necessary to phone the doctor when a child is ill, provided he is consulted immediately certain alarming symptoms appear. In the list below, the symptoms calling for speedy contact with the family doctor are marked with a ★. In the case of an accident, this ★ means that the child must be rushed to the casualty department of a hospital. In the remaining cases (marked with a ■) it will be all right to wait until the doctor's surgery is open.

Fevers
★ when the temperature, after being high at first, drops and then rises again;
★ when a child has a high temperature and looks very ill;
★ when a rise in temperature is accompanied by infantile convulsions, although the child has never had them before;
★ when a child suffers several fits of convulsions in succession, or suffers a fit lasting more than 10–15 minutes;
★ when a child with a high temperature complains of a headache and a stiff neck;
★ when, for some unknown reason, a child has been running a temperature of more than 102° Fahrenheit (39°C) for more than 3 or 4 days.

Colds
★ when breathing difficulties occur;
■ when the child is suffering from severe earache

Stomach-ache
★ when a child with stomach-ache vomits, and if his temperature rises;
★ when a child, especially one under the age of three years, is suffering from severe gripes every 5–10 minutes;
★ when a child has a pain on the right side of his abdomen, feels sick and will not stand up straight;

★ when a child complains of pain in the groin, especially when the groin is swollen;
★ when a child is feverish and has a pain in the back over the kidneys;
★ when a child keeps vomiting.

Measles
■ when the temperature remains high for longer than 4 days after the rash appears, or when there are other signs of complications.

Mumps
■ when a child suddenly gets a headache and a high temperature just as the illness seems to be over;
■ when there are indications that a boy's testicles are inflamed (see page 47).

Whooping-cough
■ when a child is under two years old.

Possible disease of the urinary passages
■ when a child has repeated rises in temperature without any other symptoms;
■ when a child experiences a smarting sensation on passing water, and when urination occurs with unusual frequency;
■ when a child's urine is red or reddish brown, as though it contains blood.

Poisoning
★ when a child has eaten or drunk something that could be poisonous.

Injuries
★ when the wound is deep (e.g., a stab-wound) or when the wound is dirty;
★ when the wound is a large one with gaping edges;
★ when the wound causes serious loss of blood;
★ when a child has a big wound and it is not certain that he is effectively

protected against tetanus;
★ when a deep wound has been made by the bite of a dog, horse, cat, rat or human being.

Burns
★ when the burn is on the face, joints or hands and feet;
★ in third-degree burns (see page 72) or when burns cover more than 2 per cent of the surface of the body;
★ in small burns when the child is in pain or has other symptoms of infection.

Adverse effects of cold
★ when feeling and the normal body temperature are not restored after 30 minutes;
★ when chilblains or frostbite produce blisters;
★ when there is a general reduction in body temperature (see page 75).

Eye injuries
★ when the eye has been damaged by a sharp object;
★ when acid or alkali, etc. has been splashed into the eye;
★ when a child is suffering from pain or from blurred vision after a blow on the eye.

Head injuries
★ when a child complains of a headache and feels dizzy and sick.

Back injuries
★ when a child feels a stabbing pain in the back, or a pricking or tingling sensation in the legs, or the legs have no feeling.

Sprains
■ when the pain and swelling do not subside within a few days;
■ when a child is in severe pain, when the foot swells up and the skin changes colour.

★ **Fractures and dislocations of the bones**

★ **Snake-bites**

Bee and wasp stings
★ when a child is allergic to them.

Whom to phone

It is important to know where to turn when a child is suddenly taken ill and needs urgent attention or has had an accident. Important numbers should be written down and kept by the phone. In *serious accidents* go to the casualty department of the nearest hospital, or if you do not live near a hospital, the nearest doctor's surgery. In severe cases of *acute illness* you must go to the nearest hospital with a children's ward or to the nearest doctor. If *the symptoms are not acute* ring the local health centre or clinic for advice. The staff usually know which children's diseases are going round at the time. When the family doctor has a surgery of his own it is usually best to phone him there. If *specialist help* is required your own doctor will give you a letter of introduction.

What should the doctor know?

The doctor's job will be made easier if you can answer the following questions as accurately as possible:

If the child has a fever, and if its onset has been quick or slow, and if the temperature has gone up and down or has remained constant;

If the child has other symptoms – e.g., vomiting, diarrhoea, stomach-ache, headache, a rash, difficulty in breathing, lassitude;

If other members of the family have the illness, and if the illness is going round the nursery or school.

Important phone numbers

Health Centre or clinic . . .
Casualty department at the hospital . . .
The Doctor . . .

Addresses

Association for all Speech-impaired Children
Room 14, Toynbee Hall
28 Commercial Street
London E1 6LS
Tel. 01-247 1497

Asthma Research Council
12 Pembridge Square
London W2 4EH
Tel. 01-229 1149

British Diabetic Association
10 Queen Anne Street
London WC1M 0BD
Tel. 01-323 1531

The British Epilepsy Association
Crowthorne House
New Wokingham Road
Wokingham, Berkshire
Tel. Crowthorne (03446) 3122

The Coeliac Society
PO Box 181
London NW2 2QY

The Cystic Fibrosis Research Trust
5 Blyth Road
Bromley
Kent BR1 3RS
Tel. 01-464 7211

Invalid Children's Aid Association
126 Buckingham Palace Road
London SW1W 9SB
Tel. 01-730 9891

Migraine Trust
45 Great Ormond Street
London WC1N 3HD
Tel 01-278 2676

National Association for the Welfare of Children in Hospital
Exton House
7 Exton Street
London SE1 8VE
Tel. 01-261 1738

National Deaf Children's Society
31 Gloucester Place
London W1H 4EA
Tel. 01-486 3251

National Eczema Society
5 Tavistock Place
London WC1H 9SR
Tel. 01-388 4097

Royal National Institute for the Blind (RNIB)
224 Great Portland Street
London W1N 6AA
Tel. 01-388 1266

Royal Society for the Prevention of Accidents (RoSPA)
Cannon House
The Priory
Queensway
Birmingham B4 6BS
Tel. 021-223 2461

Fever

Small children are quite liable to rises in temperature without being really ill. Their temperature can rise when they have been playing energetically in hot weather. Children suffer from high temperatures more readily than do adults, and their temperatures rise more quickly.

A child's temperature fluctuates between 97·5° and 99·5°F (36·5° and 37·5°C). The temperature is lowest at night when the child is asleep and is highest at noon. You should make a note of your child's normal temperature range so that you can tell whether or not he has a fever.

Usually a fever is caused by some infection such as the common cold, a stomach 'bug' or a bladder infection. A rise in temperature is one sign that the body is fighting bacteria or viruses.

Often, in addition to a rise in temperature, the child displays other symptoms which will give a clue as to the nature of the trouble. When an infant below the age of three years has a sudden high temperature, roseola infantum is the first thing to think of (see page 50). Serious infections such as meningitis can start in the same way, but other symptoms quickly appear.

Treatment

- A feverish child usually modifies his activities of his own accord. Often he prefers to stay in bed. If he does not want to stay in bed, he is better off playing in the room than fretting over enforced rest.
- Do not dress the child in clothes that are too thick, and do not use too many bedclothes. This will make the temperature rise higher still.

- If the temperature is very high it is sometimes good to give an antipyretic (i.e., something to bring the temperature down), as the fever itself can be unpleasant and even harmful. However, do not be in too much of a hurry over this; a fever is one of the body's natural defence mechanisms against infections and it is not so distressing to children as it is to adults.
- Should the child go into convulsions, or have suffered from them in the past, an antipyretic should definitely be given.
- Suitable antipyretics are those containing aspirin. Never exceed the dose stated on the packet, or what the doctor prescribes. Too many tablets can be dangerous for a child. Some children are brought out in a rash by aspirin preparations.
- If there are no suitable antipyretics in the house, the temperature can be reduced a little by sponging the child down with lukewarm water (about 86°F − 30°C).
- Above all, let the child have enough to drink, because his fluid loss is considerable and unless it is made good there is a risk of dehydration. The child must drink at least 1¼−1¾ pints of liquid per day, and even more if he is suffering from vomiting or diarrhoea. Give him lemonade, diluted fruit-juice or water sweetened with glucose − in small quantities if he is queasy. Most feverish children become thirsty and are glad to drink. However, if the child is reluctant to drink from a glass, he might like to drink through a straw. Juicy fruit and ice-creams are also useful sources of liquid.
- A feverish child usually loses his appetite. Do not force him to eat but try tempting him with small portions of his favourite food.

normal temperature

The reading on this thermometer is 'normal', or 36·8°C (98·6°F). Before you use the thermometer to take another temperature you must hold it at the top end and shake it with quick flicks of the wrist until the thread of mercury has disappeared.

Cold food and drink are often easier to manage. Ice-cream is usually welcomed, and in addition to its food value has a cooling effect.

- A temperature chart should be kept. This will provide the doctor with useful information about the course of the disease if he has to be called.
- It is sometimes necessary to take a sick child to the doctor. Wrap him in a blanket and drive him in the car. A child with a very high fever should not be heavily wrapped.

Notifying the doctor

The doctor must be notified when the following symptoms appear:

- when the child's temperature has exceeded 102°F (39°C) for more than three or four days;
- when the temperature falls and then rises again;
- when the child is running a high temperature, is listless and refuses to drink;
- when the child complains of a stiff neck and a headache while running a high temperature. But remember that children with these symptoms can be very ill even without a high temperature.

For convulsions see page 60.

How to take the temperature

Shake the mercury down after the thermometer has been used (and check that it has been shaken down before use). The correct procedure is to hold the top of the thermometer with a firm grip and to shake it downward in the air with quick flicks of the wrist until the thread of mercury is scarcely visible.

Do not put the thermometer in the mouth as the child may bite off the end. It is best to take the temperature under the armpit, with the child's arm held against the body for two minutes. You can also take it in the back passage as shown in the pictures below. Grease the stub-end with a little petroleum jelly (Vaseline) so that it will slide in easier.

Babies. Lay the infant on his back. Lift his legs up with one hand and with the other carefully push the stub of the thermometer into his back passage. Keep hold of his feet until the thermometer has been removed after the mercury stops rising.

Toddlers. Lay the child on his stomach on your lap and keep firm hold of his feet with your left hand.

Toddlers who struggle. Lay the child face down on your lap and grip his legs between your thighs to stop him kicking.

The thermometer must be cleaned after use. First shake it down and then wash it with soap and lukewarm water. Use a disinfectant if available. Alternatively, temperature strips are available. These are placed on the child's forehead and in a few minutes the letter N (normal) or F (fever) will appear. You will quickly learn to sense whether your child has a high temperature or not. There is no need to take the temperature in the case of normal uncomplicated colds.

How to take the temperatures of babies and toddlers.

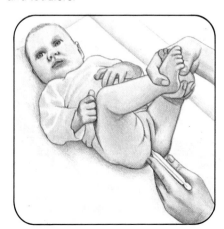
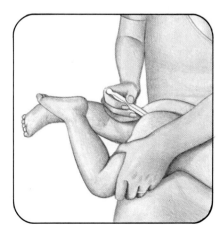

The air-passages

Infections of the upper air-passages are the commonest of acute infectious diseases, including above all the common cold. A cold begins behind the nose high up in the pharynx, in the so-called lymphatic tissue connecting the nose and pharynx.

In some children who are subject to colds, this lymphatic tissue is permanently enlarged to give what are known as *swollen adenoids*. Sometimes the nose alone is infected and there is a runny nose and sneezing, or perhaps the infection is confined to the pharynx, in which case the temperature rises slightly and swallowing becomes difficult; babies with this condition often keep crying and have little appetite.

When the palatine tonsils – generally known as 'the' tonsils – are red and swollen and have white patches on them, the child is suffering from *tonsillitis* or *quinsy*.

An infection can spread from the nasal cavities to the nasal sinuses, which are air-filled cavities lined with mucous membrane and excavated in the bones of the face. The result is the condition known as *sinusitis*. Sinuses are found in the superior maxillary bones under the eyes and in the frontal bone over the nose; there are two more sinuses behind the back of the nose and others in the skull behind the nasal cavity. The canals between the nose and the sinuses easily become blocked during a cold; the usual secretions of the sinuses are unable to drain away, and become a breeding-ground for bacteria. During infancy the sinuses develop slowly, so before the child starts school sinusitis is rare.

The infection can spread from the pharynx via the Eustachian tube to the middle ear and set up *inflammation* and *earache*.

When the infection penetrates deeper into the air-passages it reaches that part of the throat housing the vocal cords, and, if inflammation occurs here the tissues become swollen and allow the passage of only a small air-stream. The child then shows the characteristic symptoms of *croup*: hoarseness and difficulty in breathing.

Should the infection move further until it reaches the bronchi, the child gets *bronchitis*. The cough is persistent, and phlegm is brought up.

If the infection reaches the lung tissues via the bloodstream or through the trachea, *pneumonia* can follow with a high fever, heavy coughing, difficulty in breathing and sometimes pain in the chest.

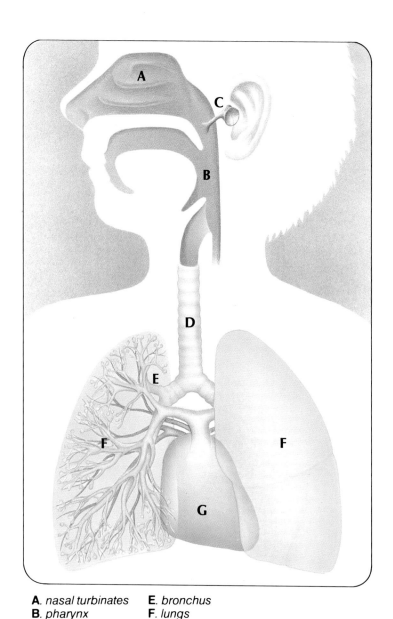

A. *nasal turbinates*
B. *pharynx*
C. *Eustachian tube*
D. *trachea*
E. *bronchus*
F. *lungs*
G. *heart*

The common cold

Children are very susceptible to infections of the air-passages, with a clogged nose, coughing and a sore throat. They catch cold much more often than adults do and five to six colds a year is quite normal. In most instances the cold is caused by a virus (see page 18). A chill does not necessarily result in a cold, but it lowers an individual's resistance to disease, and an inflammation of the upper parts of the air-passages (a cold) is more likely to occur.

Contagiousness

The viruses responsible for colds are very contagious, because they are conveyed in the droplets sprayed into the atmosphere by coughing and sneezing (droplet infection). It is virtually impossible to protect children against infection when they come in contact with other children. The risk of infection is greatest during the incubation period – i.e., before there are any obvious symptoms; a child can already have infected his playmates before anyone knows he has a cold. Children often catch cold in autumn and winter, when they spend more time indoors, and their resistance is lower than in summer. Babies are not so liable to catch cold during their first six months, because they enjoy a certain degree of immunity from the antibodies received from their mothers. Breast-fed babies are even better protected against the virus of the common cold. After the first few months the child starts to build up his own resistance, and after some years colds become less frequent. However, no one ever obtains a genuine immunity from colds.

The course of a cold

A cold can break out a few hours or a few days after a child has been infected; usually the incubation period is 1–3 days. Sometimes the child has no more than a stuffy nose and is rather tired. In this case there is hardly any rise in temperature. On the other hand, he can be really unwell for a few days, with a temperature of up to 102·5°F (39°C) plus a headache, a cold in the nose, a sore throat and sore muscles. All varieties are possible. There can even be a rash that looks like German measles.

Generally speaking, the infection lasts no longer than 5–6 days and disappears without further complications. If it lingers a bacterial infection has probably taken over.

Treatment

- Usually there is no need for the child to stay in bed, but he should be kept in restful surroundings.
- Often the rise in temperature is so slight that nothing need be given for it. However, an aspirin-based remedy may be given if the child has a tendency to convulsions.
- Give the child plenty to drink if he is feverish, in order to replace the fluid lost.
- If the child has a blocked nose, make it easier for him to breathe by propping his head up with extra pillows. This will also reduce the risk of earache.
- If the nose is badly blocked, ask the doctor for some nasal drops.
- When the child has an irritating dry cough, which can be especially troublesome at night, a cough medicine will often help – e.g., phenergan expectorant. When the cough is loose but the phlegm is difficult to bring up, use a recommended linctus.
- Smear a little protecting ointment under a runny nose.
- When the temperature has come down and the child has recuperated, he can return to school, even when he still has a cough or his nose is still running. At this stage he can no longer infect others.

The prevention of colds

There is no sure-fire vaccine against the common cold, but the child is less susceptible if he is in good condition – if he has good food to eat, has adequate sound sleep and gets plenty of fresh air. Children whose environment contains tobacco-smoke are much more easily infected than children living in a smoke-free environment. But the susceptibility varies from one child to another and from one time of life to another.

Swollen adenoids can cause repeated infections, but they can be removed by a simple operation.

Notifying the doctor

The doctor must be notified if the following symptoms appear:
- if the child runs a high temperature for more than 3 or 4 days or is very unlike his usual self;
- if the fever falls for a few days only to rise again;
- if a complication such as inflammation of the ear (page 20) or of the sinuses (page 17) is suspected.

A cold in the head
(rhinitis)

A stuffy nose can be quite uncomfortable for very small children because they do not yet know the right way to breathe through their mouth. For this reason it can become difficult for them to feed at the breast or to drink from a bottle when they catch a cold. In this severe case it will be easier for them when their head is propped up or when they are sitting semi-erect.

Treatment

- When the nose is very blocked up, nasal drops – obtainable on prescription – will often help.
- When the nasal discharge – which was at first thin and clear – becomes thick and yellow-green, and the child becomes feverish, you must get in touch with the doctor. The child may be suffering from sinusitis or some other bacterial infection behind the nose for which antibiotics are required.

Enlarged adenoids

At the back and top of the pharynx there is a considerable amount of lymphatic tissue which resists the spread of infection towards the ears. This sometimes swells so that the child has difficulty in breathing through the nose. Swollen adenoids generally occur in children between the ages of three and five. After this period the tissue shrinks and the symptoms disappear. A child with adenoids sounds as if his nose is blocked and he goes round with his mouth open. He snores at night and when he goes to bed in the evening and wakes up in the morning he often suffers from an irritative cough.

Enlarged adenoids can even be the cause of earache, because they can partially close the Eustachian tube.

Treatment

When the adenoids are swollen and the child often suffers from earache and sore throats, an operation can be performed. The adenoids are removed in hospital under anaesthetic. Usually the child can return home the same day.

Sore throat
(tonsillitis)

In this disease the tonsils are inflamed. The inflammation is usually caused by streptococci, the same type of bacteria as in scarlet fever. Children are seldom troubled by it before their second year.

Tonsillitis is infectious, and the bacteria are spread when the child coughs.

The child has a very sore throat and complains that it hurts to swallow. The tonsils look red and swollen, and often have white patches on them. The voice sounds hoarse. Sometimes the lymph glands in the angle of the jaw can be swollen too. There is a temperature of 102–104°F (39–40°C) for some three to four days. Small children will vomit fairly frequently. If there are no complications they usually recover after a week.

Treatment

- The child should be given antibiotics. These will usually consist of penicillin, and should be given by the doctor. The symptoms will then subside within a few days.
- As long as the child is running a temperature, he must be kept quiet. However, he should stay in bed only if he wishes to do so. When his temperature has returned to normal he may be up and about as usual and may even go out of doors, but must not return to school until his temperature has been normal for a few days.
- Eating and drinking is often uncomfortable, because swallowing is difficult. Cold, liquid food like ice-cream is usually best.

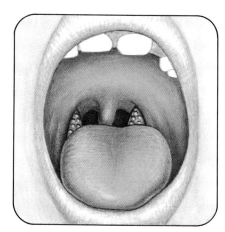

With a sore throat, the tonsils are red and swollen and often have white patches on them.

Cough

The fact that a child has a cough can be due to any one of a number of infections of the air-passages. When the infection is in the larynx the cough sounds hoarse, whereas a tracheal cough is dry and wheezing. If the infection is lower down in the air-passages – i.e., in the bronchi – the cough is often loose and phlegm is brought up. Enlargement of the adenoids (see page 16) can cause a tedious irritative cough, especially on going to bed and when waking up. An irritative cough may be an allergic reaction, and in this case it is often associated with a whistling sound as the child breathes.

Treatment

- There are two kinds of cough medicine: one allays the irritation and the other loosens the phlegm. Very small children must not be given cough medicines.
- Sometimes lukewarm lemonade (made from freshly squeezed lemons and sweetened with honey) is all that is required to release the mucus and to relieve the cough.
- For whooping-cough see page 48.

Bronchitis

An ordinary cold can lead to bronchitis if the infection travels down the trachea to the bronchi. The disease can also occur as a complication in measles and whooping-cough or as an independent infection.

The child suffers from a persistent cough and his sleep is disturbed. The mucus sounds as if it is 'bubbling' in the chest, and the whole rib-cage seems to vibrate. The child tends to swallow the phlegm after a coughing fit rather than to spit it out.

The temperature fluctuates but seldom rises above 100°F (38°C). Usually the child has lost his appetite and is tired and listless.

Treatment

- Keep the child quietly indoors for a few days.
- Give an expectorant to liquefy the mucus, as advised by the doctor or chemist.
- Call the doctor: if the temperature remains high for longer than 3–4 days; when the temperature rises and the child seems to be having some difficulty in breathing; when the cough does not get better. Pneumonia can develop, or the bronchitis may need to be treated with antibiotics.

Sinusitis

The sinuses in the bones of the face are air-filled cavities coated with mucous membrane and connected with the nasal cavity by small openings. An originally slight infection can lead to inflammation of the sinuses (especially the frontal and paranasal sinuses) if it manages to spread. The already narrow openings become blocked when the mucous membrane of the nose swells up during a cold or in an allergic reaction (see page 56). Bacteria are always present in the nose, and they readily multiply in blocked sinuses. However, children do not usually suffer from sinusitis before the age of six.

The symptoms of sinusitis can be so slight as to go unnoticed. In this case there is generally no need for further treatment. However, if the nasal mucus is greenish-yellow and thick, and if the child complains of a headache at the same time, you can be almost certain that sinusitis has set in. Probably there will not be much by way of fever, although the temperature may rise to 100–102°F (38–39°C). On the other hand, the rise in temperature can be persistent, lasting for several weeks. Weariness, listlessness and loss of appetite are other typical symptoms. Sinusitis may last for some time.

Treatment

Notify the doctor. He will usually prescribe nasal drops and antibiotics. In special cases it may be necessary for the sinuses to be washed out.

Influenza

Influenza is caused by different viruses (or strains of the same virus). It occurs as epidemics, sometimes in certain regions and sometimes over the country as a whole (or over many countries, 'pandemics'). It attacks both adults and children, but children are usually not as badly affected as adults. The infection is spread by droplets floating in the atmosphere after the patient has coughed or sneezed.

The symptoms of 'flu are similar to those of a common cold, but are much more severe.

The incubation period is 1–3 days, and then the child is suddenly taken ill. He runs a high temperature of 102·5–104°F (39–40°C) and suffers from shivering fits, sore muscles and a headache. Other symptoms are a dry cough and irritation of the eyes.

Small children can have convulsions, because the temperature rise is so fast. They can also vomit and suffer from diarrhoea. The fever usually lasts 3–5 days, after which the child starts to convalesce.

Treatment

- When the child has caught a very heavy cold you must call the doctor.
- As in any fever, it is essential for the child to have enough to drink to prevent dehydration, especially when he is suffering from diarrhoea at the same time (see page 28). Sometimes the child gets earache or catches pneumonia. The doctor must always be notified in such cases, for these diseases have to be treated with antibiotics.
- Children with chronic lung complaints or heart trouble should be inoculated against the disease when a 'flu epidemic is on the way.

Pneumonia

If a child has a cold and the temperature does not return to normal, or else drops and then suddenly rises again, the possibility of pneumonia must be considered. This can be caused either by viruses or by bacteria – e.g., pneumococci. Other symptoms are a frequent short cough, hurried breathing, sometimes pain in the chest and a high temperature. However, pneumonia need not be preceded by a cold.

Very small children can have pneumonia without a high temperature or a pain in the chest. However, they are tired and listless and lose weight.

Virus pneumonia (atypical pneumonia) is often associated with a troublesome irritative cough, but the other symptoms are less serious than those of the pneumonia caused by bacteria. Since antibiotics have become available, pneumonia is not as dangerous as it used to be, and it occurs less frequently.

Treatment

- If ever you suspect that your child may have pneumonia, you must call the doctor; he will then prescribe antibiotics and a cough medicine if necessary.
- Give something to bring down the temperature (see page 12) if the fever distresses the child or if he is liable to convulsions (see page 60).
- Give him plenty to drink in order to replace the lost fluids.
- If he finds eating difficult give him small portions of semi-liquid food such as ice-cream.

Viruses

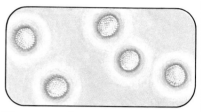

Viruses can live and multiply in living cells, where they behave as parasites and destroy the tissues. Most infectious diseases are caused by viruses. Antibiotics are ineffective against viruses, although some virus diseases such as polio and influenza can be prevented by vaccination. Viruses are much smaller than bacteria, and only the largest forms are visible under the light microscope.

Bacteria

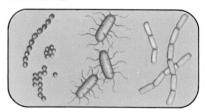

Bacteria are single-cell organisms which multiply by fission. Many of them are important to human life; the bacterial flora of the intestines, for example, are necessary to the digestive processes. Some bacteria cause disease by breaking down the tissues or by producing poisonous substances. Effective remedies – in particular antibiotics such as penicillin – are available against most of the known harmful (pathogenic) bacteria.

Croup

Croup used to be a serious complication in diphtheria, a disease that has practically died out. Today, it is an inflammation of the larynx that occurs usually in children of 1–5 years old. It usually starts with a cold, especially in autumn and early spring. Some allergic children are easily affected, sometimes even several times a year. The essential feature of the illness is a swelling of the mucous membranes below the vocal cords, so that the passage is constricted.

The course of the illness

The child can go to sleep feeling well or perhaps with a slight head-cold and then wake up in the night with a hoarse, painful barking cough. He may find breathing difficult, his chest feels tight, and he is restless. Inhaling is particularly taxing, and is often accompanied by a rattling sound. Exhaling is easier. On occasions, breathing can be so difficult that the child is in danger of suffocating (the blood cannot get enough oxygen). In this case he must be rushed to hospital without delay. Generally speaking, however, the attacks are so slight that if you recognize the symptoms and have an effective medicine ready to hand, the child can easily be helped at home. Croup can sometimes be mistaken for *bronchial asthma*, which also causes shortness of breath, but then the child does not have such a hoarse, barking cough. Both diseases can even occur at the same time. In addition there is another but very rare disease that can be confused with croup, and that is *epiglottitis*. The difference is that in epiglottitis the swelling is located in the epiglottis. This disease occurs mainly in children of 4–7 years and develops quickly without the symptoms of a common cold. The child does not cough but finds difficulty in drawing breath. He complains of a sore throat and finds most relief in sitting erect with his head bent forward. Usually he dribbles saliva out of the corners of his mouth. This is a very dangerous condition and the child must be kept in a sitting position and taken to the hospital straight away.

Treatment

- Take the child on your lap and try to calm him. Because he is finding breathing so difficult, he quickly starts to panic, and the more he screams and kicks the worse the shortage of oxygen becomes. If you can persuade the child to be quiet and relaxed he will notice that breathing becomes much easier again.
- Inhaling water vapour, preferably cold, is a well-tried method of giving relief. If you have a humidifier it can be very useful.
- An attack may also be alleviated by letting the bath fill up with hot water (preferably from the shower) and sitting the child on your lap in the bathroom for him to breathe in the 'steam'.
- Try to get the child to drink a drop of something cold such as fruit-juice or water.
- If the child is subject to attacks of croup whenever he catches a cold you may be able to get something from the doctor for reducing the swelling.
- It will be obvious when breathing returns to normal and is quiet again; nevertheless, let the child sleep propped up in a half-sitting position for the rest of the night.

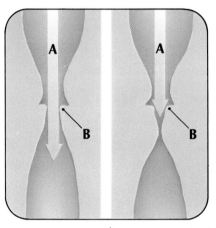

When the mucous membranes under the vocal cords swell, the air passage becomes so narrow that the child finds it hard to breathe.

A. inhaled air; **B**. vocal cords.

Notifying the doctor

The doctor must be notified when the following symptoms appear:
- when the complaint does not respond to the suggested treatments;
- when the child is in great distress right from the start and has blue lips and nails due to oxygen shortage;
- when the child is suffering an attack of croup for the first time.

- **if the child is very short of breath it is useful to give artificial respiration by mouth-to-mouth resuscitation (see page 84).**

The ear

The ear is made up of three parts: the external ear, the middle ear and the internal ear.

The *external ear* consists of the *auricle* and the *auditory canal*. The auricle extends to the *tympanic membrane* (or eardrum), which divides the external ear from the middle ear.

The *middle ear* consists of small air-filled cavities in the temporal bone lined with mucous membrane. The largest, the tympanic cavity, contains the three bones of hearing, the *malleus*, the *incus* and the *stapes*. The tympanic cavity is linked to the pharynx by a small passage called the *Eustachian tube*.

The *internal ear* contains the fluid-filled *cochlea*. Inside the cochlea are auditory cells which send messages to the hearing centre in the brain, where the signals are received and interpreted. The internal ear also contains the three semicircular canals which control our sense of balance.

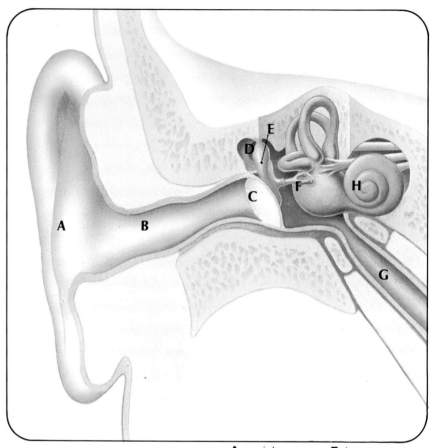

A. *auricle*	E. *incus*
B. *auditory canal*	F. *stapes*
C. *eardrum*	G. *Eustachian tube*
D. *malleus*	H. *cochlea*

Inflammation of the ear
(otitis)

Little children are very susceptible to earache. This is usually part of an ordinary cold and is not serious. However, children who have been suffering from measles or some other infectious disease that has really lowered their resistance can have inflammation of the ear as a complication.

Some children regularly have earache without any other symptoms, especially in winter. When they reach school age they are less subject to the complaint, because the Eustachian tube is bigger and they have more resistance to infections.

Inflammation of the ear is caused by bacteria which enter the middle ear through the Eustachian tube. As the mucous membrane swells the Eustachian tube becomes blocked, and the bacteria trapped in the middle ear begin to multiply. This is especially likely to happen in small children with enlarged adenoids.

When the mucous membrane is inflamed it produces more fluid. The Eustachian tube silts up at times during a cold, and fluid can accumulate in the middle ear without the presence of bacteria; this is often just as painful as a purulent ear infection. The hearing is sometimes muffled for a week or even longer after an earache.

The course of the illness

It is sometimes difficult to tell whether or not a baby has earache. The infant may be feverish and will not stop crying, but displays no other symptoms. What you can do is to press very cautiously with your finger on the auditory canal. If the eardrum is inflamed the baby will react to the pain by crying hard.

Slightly bigger children, who are still not old enough to say what is the matter, will keep rubbing their ear or turning their head from one side to the other. They cry incessantly, and are restless.

Earache is usually very intense, and without treatment can last for days. The pain is the result of excessive pressure in the middle ear, due to the fact that (possibly purulent) matter has collected immediately behind the eardrum, which is red and bulging. Occasionally it ruptures after a few hours, and the matter runs out of the auditory canal. This usually relieves the pain.

Earache generally starts in the evening when the child has been sleeping for a short while. This is because it is easier for the Eustachian tube to become blocked when the child is lying in bed.

Inflammation of the ear is often accompanied by a rise in temperature to 100–102°F (38–39°C) and sometimes even higher. But inflammation of the ear may occur without a rise in temperature or earache.

Treatment

- Inflammation of the ear is usually treated with antibiotics and nasal drops. Always notify the doctor; if the inflammation is not properly treated the hearing may be permanently impaired.
- If the earache occurs in the evening or at night the following measures may be taken if the child is not too poorly, and you can wait till morning before calling the doctor.
- Let the child lie with his head propped up. This in itself can help to reduce the pain.
- Give a junior aspirin or something similar to ease the pain. Nasal drops to reduce the swelling of the mucous membrane will give quick relief if administered correctly (see page 109). Should the child be subject to earache, keep the nasal drops in the house. A mild earache is often better the next day when these steps are taken.

- An inflammation of the ear accompanied by an accumulation of pus usually clears up in 7–10 days when treated with penicillin.
- It is important to have the child's hearing tested after this treatment.
- At one time the eardrum was often pricked in inflammation of the ear, in order to relieve the pressure and to take away the pain. Doctors tend to avoid this nowadays unless the accumulation of matter in the middle ear will not disperse. Sometimes the eardrum perforates spontaneously.
- A recent method for preventing recurrent inflammation of the ear is an operation in which a tiny plastic tube is inserted in the eardrum. This keeps the middle ear drained and dry, and repeated earache can no longer occur. Unfortunately, the operation does not help all children.

Complications

Repeated inflammation of the ear or an earache that is neglected can lead to permanently impaired hearing. Take your child to the doctor if you think he does not hear properly.

Ear-wax

In the auditory canal there are glands which secrete wax. Usually the ear-wax oozes out into the auricle and can be removed when the ears are washed, but in some children who have a narrow auditory canal the wax can form a plug.

Treatment

- Since a plug of ear-wax can impair a child's hearing, it has to be removed. Consult the doctor.
- Never poke anything into a child's ear. The auditory canal is sensitive, and the extremely vulnerable middle ear is easily damaged.

The eye

The eye is covered by the *conjunctiva*, a thin transparent membrane that also covers the inside of the eyelid. Underneath this membrane lies the white, opaque, hard *selera*. The transparent *cornea* at the front of the eye refracts light-rays.

Under the cornea lies the coloured part known as the *iris*. This contains the muscles which open and shut the pupil. The *pupil* is the small dark aperture through which light-rays enter the interior of the eye.

Behind the pupil lies the *lens*. The muscles of the lens can modify its shape in such a way as to throw beams of light from different objects on the light-sensitive *retina*. Here the image of what is being looked at is formed and then transmitted to the brain via the optic nerve. The brain makes us conscious of what we see.

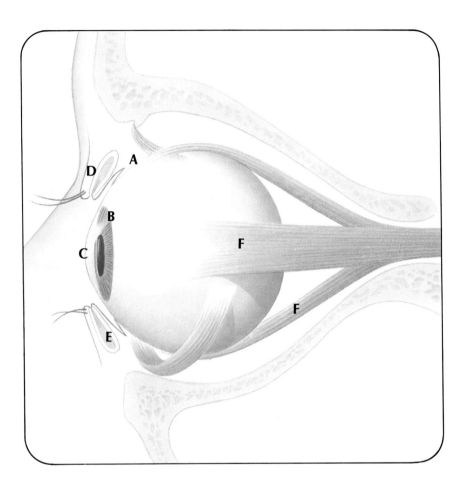

A. *conjunctiva*
B. *iris*
C. *pupil*
D. *eyelid*
E. *tear gland*
F. *muscles of the eye*

Conjunctivitis

The conjunctiva covering the inside of the eyelid can become inflamed by an infection, or because the eye has been irritated by some chemical or the like. For example, cold viruses easily spread through the fine tear-duct linking the eye and the nose.

Children with a tendency to hay fever (see page 56) often get sore eyes when they catch a cold. The eyes become red and irritated, and they itch and smart.

Treatment

Dry the child's eyes with a compress or with a flannel moistened with lukewarm water. Do not use cotton-wool. Usually the inflammation subsides spontaneously. However, if it fails to do so, ask the doctor to prescribe eye drops or an ointment.

Sties

A sty in the eye is caused by an infection at the root of an eyelash. Some people suffer a good deal from sties. However, the sty will disappear of its own accord in a few days more often than not.

Consult the doctor if the sty causes much discomfort or if the child is subject to sties.

Defects of vision

If a child complains about pain in his eyes you must notify the doctor. The doctor must also be consulted if a child holds a book too close to his eyes or often tilts his head when looking at something. Visual defects can also cause headaches.

The most common defects involving the way in which the eye refracts light are hyperopia or hypermetropia (far-sightedness), astigmatism and myopia (near-sightedness). These defects are often hereditary, and can lead to squinting.

Hyperopia comes about because the eyeball is too short. Because the light-rays come to a focus behind the retina, the small muscles of the eye are strained when the eye is trying to look at something near at hand. This can be helped by wearing convex lenses.

Astigmatism means that the light-rays are focused unevenly on the retina. Because of this, the images of objects are deformed. A round object, for example, will look oval. Specially ground spectacle lenses can correct this defect.

Myopia usually occurs at school age, but children who were premature at birth are often myopic from the start. In myopia the eyeball is too long and the light-rays come to a focus in front of the retina. Near objects look distinct, but distant objects look blurred. Near-sightedness can be corrected with concave lenses.

Colour-blindness in its commonest form is the inability to distinguish between red and green, but there are also other forms. It may be difficult to decide whether or not a child is colour-blind because small children are not always sure of the names of colours. Only when they reach the age of four can you be certain how well they distinguish between them.

Squint
(strabismus)

Squinting mainly arises because the nerve control of the eye muscles is poor. Far-sightedness and astigmatism are often causes.

In a child with normal vision the images from both eyes are blended into a single image in the brain. When a child squints, however, the brain has to cope with two separate images. It selects one and switches 'off' the eye supplying the other. Without remedial training, the child could lose the ability to see with that eye.

A baby can see at birth. A few weeks later he will stare at an object 8 inches (200mm) away, but sometimes, especially when he is tired, he rolls one eye only to look at an object – this is because the eye muscles are still not sufficiently strong.

At 3 months he should be able to adapt his gaze. If one eye squints, or if he still has difficulty in focusing on an object, he should be taken to the clinic for examination.

Treatment

It is important to get advice on your child if you think he is squinting. The sooner treatment is started the better: at the age of one year proper vision can be fully restored.
- In squinting the weakest eye has to be trained and various methods are employed to make it work. Usually the sound eye is covered with a patch from time to time, and if there are problems of refraction, spectacles are also prescribed.
- On the other hand, corrective operations for squint are more in vogue nowadays than they used to be.
- Another method that has met with success is the so-called orthoptic exercises: the child must try to use both eyes and to achieve binocular vision. But the child must be at least 3 or 4 years old so that he can cooperate.

The stomach and intestines

The system by which our food is reduced to particles small enough to be taken into the bloodstream is a complicated one. What we eat is broken down with the help of various chemicals (e.g., enzymes) present in saliva, gastric juices and intestinal juices.

The food is masticated in the *mouth* by the teeth and is mixed with saliva from the salivary glands. The saliva helps the food to slip more easily into the oesophagus (or gullet).

After the small pieces of food have been forced via the pharynx into the *oesophagus* a wave of muscle movements carries them into the stomach. In the mucous membrane of the *stomach* there are glands which among other things secrete hydrochloric acid and enzymes to convert the food into a fairly smooth pulp.

The contents of the stomach are then passed, little by little, into the small intestine. The final breaking down of the food takes place in the first section of the small intestine, the duodenum. It is in this section that the bile and pancreatic juice enter through their respective ducts.

Bile is manufactured in the liver, and one of its functions is to emulsify fats. The *pancreas* supplies pancreatic juice containing enzymes which digest proteins, fats and carbohydrates. Partly in the duodenum, but mainly in the following section of the *small intestine*, the digested food is absorbed by the intestinal villi. These millions of tiny, tuft-like organs contain blood vessels and lymph vessels which convey the nutrients to the various parts of the body.

Where the small intestine passes into the large intestine we find the caecum and the vermiform appendix. In the large intestine water is extracted from the faeces, which are reduced to half their original bulk.

Finally, the contents of the intestines enter the *rectum*, and at that stage consist mainly of indigestible food residues and bacteria.

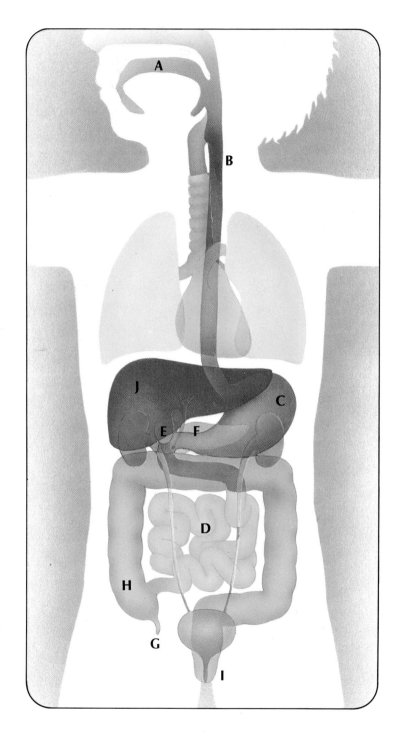

A. *oral cavity*
B. *oesophagus*
C. *stomach*
D. *small intestine*
E. *gall bladder*
F. *pancreas*
G. *appendix*
H. *large intestine*
I. *rectum*
J. *liver*

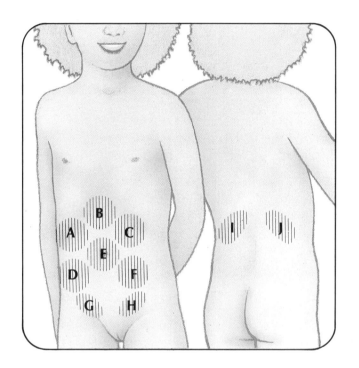

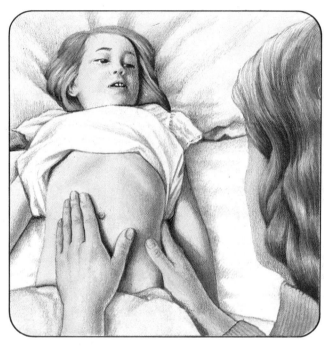

Stomach-ache

Stomach-ache is a common symptom, but its cause is often difficult to determine. It can be anything from appendicitis to ordinary indigestion. A child can often react with a pain in the abdomen when the problem (an infection say) exists elsewhere. It is not unusual for a stomach-ache to be caused by anxiety or excitement.

In *appendicitis* the pain often starts above the navel (B). Later on it is displaced to a spot lower down on the right of the abdomen (D).

The region around the navel (E) is where children frequently experience pain, especially when they are suffering from *gastric influenza* or *have eaten something that has disagreed with them*, or have *umbilical colic*.

Pain in the region of the spleen (C) is very unusual.

In some *intestinal infections* the discomfort is located on the left side of the abdomen (F).

An *inguinal hernia* can give pain in the groin (G and H), which will be found to be specially tender when pressed gently with the fingers.

Back pain (I and J) can be caused by the kidneys, and could indicate *pyelitis*.

Gallstones and *cholecystitis* (inflammation of the gall-bladder) are very rare in children. If they do occur, the pain is at the top right of the abdomen (A). The pain often radiates round to the back (above J).

How to examine a child

A child may find it very hard to say just where he has a pain. You can help to locate the pain by pressing carefully on his abdomen. When the doctor comes you can describe the symptoms. Let the child lie on his back in bed in as relaxed a position as possible with his knees slightly bent and his arms at his sides. Make sure that your hands are not cold. Sometimes children dislike this examination so much that they tense up and the abdomen feels hard. Start by pressing cautiously at first and then somewhat harder on the area around the navel and then press in the same way on other places on the abdomen. Keep your eye on the child all the time to see if he reacts.

Appendicitis

Where the small intestine passes into the large intestine, the latter forms a pouch known as the caecum to which a vermiform appendix is attached. This can become inflamed to give appendicitis, although seldom in children younger than 3–4 years.

The course of the illness

The first symptom is usually nausea. Then follows abdominal pain, starting above the navel more often than not and slowly moving to the right lower edge of the abdomen not far from the navel. (However, a child can only pinpoint this typical displacement of the pain when he is about 9 or 10 years old.) Afterwards the nausea increases, and the child will no longer eat or drink. Sometimes he vomits. In the beginning the fever is moderate: 99·5–100·5°F (37·5–38°C). The child often walks bending forward.

The course of the disease can vary from case to case. Generally, the abdominal pain becomes very severe within a few days and the temperature rises to around 102·5°F (39°C). However, a child can also have appendicitis without a high temperature. It is *possible* for the only symptoms to be a slight nausea and abdominal pain.

Take the temperature every two hours if you suspect appendicitis. A combination of slowly rising temperature, nausea and abdominal pain is particularly alarming. Always notify the doctor or the hospital in such a case.

Treatment

A blood test or an X-ray examination will not yield a completely reliable diagnosis. However, if the doctor thinks that appendicitis is likely he will arrange for an operation to be performed to remove the appendix. The operation is a simple one, and the child will probably be back home in a few days.

Complications

If the inflamed appendix is not taken out it can burst after some days; the pus will be released, and spread through the whole abdomen. When the appendix bursts the pain is relieved but the temperature rises, the abdomen becomes hard and sensitive and the child feels very exhausted. Appendicitis can be difficult to distinguish from intestinal colic, but even here an operation may be required as quickly as possible.

Intussusception

Intussusception is a condition found mainly in children under two years old. One part of the intestine is pushed into another so that the intestinal tract is squeezed and the faeces are unable to pass. The blood supply to the intestines is also restricted.

The course of the illness

The onset of the symptoms is abrupt, and the child is seized with severe abdominal pains lasting a few minutes and recurring every 10 to 30 minutes. He cries loudly during the attacks, and turns pale. In the intervals he is a little calmer, but as soon as the pain returns he begins to cry again. If this state of affairs continues he starts shivering, begins to vomit and runs a temperature.

Treatment

Should you think your child has an intussusception call the doctor without delay. If the trouble is caught in time, the hospital staff may be able to push the bowels back into place. An operation will be necessary if this treatment is unsuccessful.

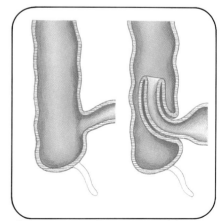

In intussusception one part of the intestine is pushed into another part.

Constipation

By constipation we mean difficult bowel movements which occur only at intervals of several days.

Treatment

0–8 months. Breast-fed infants seldom suffer from constipation even when the motion is delayed for a few days or even a week.

- If a bottle-fed child has a stoppage, check whether you are using the correct quantities when preparing the feeds.
- A baby can react to a change of feed with a stoppage. Give him time to get used to the new feed and do not be in too much of a hurry to try something else.
- If the stoppage persists, and provided the child is at least two months old (for younger children ask the health centre or clinic), you can give a few teaspoonfuls of stewed prunes (the juice and a little pulp, not the skin) or orange juice.
- If the baby is eating fruit, choose the kinds which are laxative. Greens and fruit contain fibres which counteract the binding action of milk products.

From 8 months. When children over the age of 8 months suffer from constipation this is usually the fault of their diet. It is important for them to have a varied diet with plenty of greens, fruit and wholemeal products.

- Make sure that the child is not eating food which will make him constipated, such as white bread and dishes overloaded with flour and milk. The total amount of milk consumed per day (including that used to make up soft food) should not exceed ½ litre.
- Give the child 'porridge' made with wholemeal flour.
- When the child is two years old alternate the 'porridge' with wholemeal muesli. This can occasionally be given with yoghurt.
- Give the child wholewheat bread with a slice of cheese or a slice of meat on top.
- Use yoghurt instead of ordinary milk.
- Younger children, especially, benefit from raw green salads.
- Ensure that fruit is always on the menu.
- Give the child prune juice.
- Lively children begrudge the time spent sitting on the pot or WC, while sometimes parents will try to hurry their offspring. It is important to teach a child to sit patiently on the WC at the same time each day, preferably in the morning after breakfast. Most children are not ready for toilet training before they are a year old.

Be sparing with milk products, egg, egg dishes and cheese.

Cut out white bread, food made from refined wheat flour (pancakes, spaghetti, puddings), rice, boiled milk, tea and chocolate.

Notifying the doctor

When in spite of the fact that his diet has been regulated, and he has been trained to open his bowels at the same time each day, a child is still constipated, the advice of the family doctor or of the health centre should be sought. Constipation can have some medical cause. Never give laxatives unless told to do so by the doctor.

Diarrhoea and gastric influenza

Children are rather susceptible to diarrhoea, which is usually due to an intestinal infection. With the adoption of a special diet (see page 28), the trouble is generally over in a few days. In diarrhoea the bowel movements are thin and watery, and sometimes there is severe vomiting – especially in the case of gastric influenza. Small children often have a temperature rise to between 100·4 and 102·5°F (38 and 39°C) when suffering from acute diarrhoea. Do not assume that it is a good sign when the patient seems to be settling down; it might indicate that he has lost too much fluid to react further.

Within 1 to 5 days a baby is usually well again and older children can recover even sooner. Care should be taken over what the child is given to eat for a few days. Some acute infections caused by viruses or bacteria present in the stomach can bring about diarrhoea or gastric influenza, but the same symptoms can also be produced if the child eats something bad such as tainted meat and in certain types of poisoning. Diarrhoea may also be due to an allergy or to the fact that the child is unable to digest something in the food.

Treatment for acute diarrhoea

- It is important immediately to give a child with acute diarrhoea liquids, even if he vomits, in order to make good the loss of salt and fluids. Boiled water, rice water or carrot soup are very good because they do not overburden the stomach and intestines. All that water and rice water do is to supply the needed liquid, but strained carrot soup also has a binding effect.

    When a child vomits repeatedly give him finely chopped food to eat several times a day.
- After the child's stomach has recovered he can gradually return to his normal diet over a period of two to three days. Because the mucous membrane lining the stomach is often sensitive to wheat flour after a heavy bout of diarrhoea, it is best to give gruel for a day or two. For the same reason, avoid giving the child biscuits, rusk, bread or flour products until he is completely better.
- Some children tend to have thinner bowel movements when they take fruit; so if the diarrhoea becomes worse when rice is eaten with grated apple, stop giving apple during the illness.
- If the child is not on the mend within 24 hours, or has still not recovered after a week, call in the doctor.
- In babies, diarrhoea can be a serious matter.

Always get in touch with the doctor when your baby has acute diarrhoea and his general condition deteriorates.

4–6 months	number of feeds per day	Quantity of strained carrot soup/ boiled water/ rice water per feed	Quantity of ground rice gruel per feed	Other food, beginning with small portions and gradually increasing
day one	5–6	14 T*	–	
day two	5 (–6)	10½ T	3½ T	
day three	5	7 T	2–1 T	
day four	5	2–7 T	7 T	
day five	5	3½ T	10½ T	
day six	5		14 T	

7–12 months				
day one	5–6	14 T	–	
day two	5 (–6)	10½ T	3½ T	
day three	5	9 T	2 T	
day four	5	2 T	9 T	grated apple, omelette
day five	4	3½ T	10½ T	carrot purée, grated apple, omelette, boiled fish or meat perhaps with rice

(T = tablespoonful)

7–12 months	Number of feeds per day	Quantity of strained carrot soup and/or boiled water/rice water per feed	Quantity of ground rice gruel per feed	Other food, beginning with small portions and gradually increasing
day six	4	–	14 T	carrot purée, grated apple, omelette, boiled fish or meat, perhaps with rice

One year and over

day one	5	14 T	–	
day two	5	7 T	7 T	grated apple
day three	5	3½ T	10½ T	grated apple, omelette, boiled fish
day four	5	–	14 T	carrot purée, grated apple, omelette, boiled fish or meat, perhaps with rice
day five	4	–	14 T	carrot purée, grated apple, omelette, boiled fish or meat, perhaps with rice

It is preferable to cut the food into small portions during the first few days, but make sure that the total quantity does not fall below that recommended in the table.

Recipes

Ground rice

Prepare according to the instructions on the packet, taking care to use measured quantities.

Boiled water

To 1¾ pints (1 litre) of boiled water add ½ teaspoon of salt and 4–5 level teaspoonfuls of sugar. Keep the water in a covered jug in the refrigerator.

Rice water

Boil 1 tablespoon of raw rice (not instant rice) for about 20 minutes in 1¾ pints (1 litre) of water. Pass it through a sieve and make up to ⅞ pint (½ litre) with water.

Carrot soup

Mix about 12 ounces (350 grams) of carrot purée with 16 fl.oz. (½ litre) of boiled water, add a pinch of salt and 1 level tablespoonful of granulated sugar or glucose. Squeeze in a little lemon juice if desired to improve the flavour.

Omelette

1 egg
⅓ pint (⅕ litre) of boiled milk
¼ teaspoon of salt

Beat the egg, milk and salt until they are well mixed, and pour the result into a pan with a knob of butter. Hold it for a few minutes over a gentle heat until set.

Vomiting

Children have more sensitive vomiting reflexes that do adults, and small children can vomit quite violently without being ill. With regard to babies in particular, this can be a sign of drinking too much and too greedily, but a minor illness can also be the cause. However, if the child seems dull, loses weight quickly and shows signs of dehydration such as sunken eyes and wrinkled skin, always call the doctor.

A child can vomit for the following reasons:
- 'habitual vomiting'
- acute infection – gastric influenza (page 27)
- sore throat, meningitis
- 'ketotic vomiting'
- obstruction of the intestinal canal
- appendicitis (see page 26)
- concussion of the brain
- poisoning.

Ketotic vomiting

Some children can vomit regularly when they have a slight sore throat or gastric influenza, or when they are mentally tense. They then vomit quite violently, and their breath smells of acetone. They may also have a pain in the midriff. The vomiting may persist for some days if no counter-measures are taken.

Treatment

- Give your child plenty of water in small doses mixed with a little sodium bicarbonate and sugar in order to prevent dehydration and to reduce the tendency to form acetone. By supplying carbohydrate, you will be helping get the metabolism back to normal.
- If in spite of this the child seems very exhausted, call the doctor. The child may be in need of a drip to supply fluid direct to the bloodstream.

Habitual vomiting

Some small children, usually between the ages of 5 and 10 months, vomit several times a day without being ill. Sometimes they make a game of it and make themselves sick by sticking a finger down their throat. They can also bring up little morsels of sour-smelling food because they will 'chew the cud' so to speak – i.e., bring up half-digested food from the gullet and then swallow it again.

Treatment

Have a chat with someone at the clinic. Sometimes the child is vomiting as a show of displeasure, but this is by no means always the case. The vomiting usually ceases when more solid foods are taken.

Enterospasm during the first three months

Many children suffer from colic during their first weeks of life. They cry so loudly that it can be very disturbing (especially for the parents!). Colic is completely harmless to the baby, and generally stops after he is three months old.

It is not known why some infants have attacks of colic. The kind of food they eat seems to make no difference, since breast-fed infants are as liable to the attacks as are bottle-fed ones. One definite cause is that the baby manages to swallow so much air with his drink that some is left behind when he brings up wind, and this unwanted air has to pass all the way through the long and winding alimentary canal. Some gas is also formed in the intestines. The baby cries vigorously, usually after the evening feed. Sometimes he begins to cry as soon as he has had his feed, and sometimes he has a nap first and then wakes up screaming. These crying bouts can last for hours. The baby's face turns scarlet, and he pulls his arms and legs spasmodically against his body. His abdomen feels tight, and you can hear his tummy rumbling due to the trapped air. After an attack lasting a few minutes the baby usually rests for a short time before the next attack.

Treatment

- Do not let the baby drink too quickly. See if the hole in the bottle teat is too large. If you are breast-feeding him introduce short pauses during the feed.
- Burp the baby well before putting him back in his cot. Burp him several times during the feed too.
- It sometimes helps children subject to colic if they lie on their stomachs in bed.
- When a baby lies crying he can swallow air and make the pain worse. It is better to pick him up and to let him lie on your shoulder with his knees against your chest. When he is held like this he will be able to break wind more easily.
- Rub his abdomen gently after the feed. Hold him upright or let him lie on his right side when doing this. You will soon discover whether or not he likes it.

Threadworms

When a child lies awake at night complaining of itching round the anus he probably has threadworms. This is the commonest type of intestinal worm. Threadworms are infectious both to children and to adults.

Threadworms live in the rectum, where they can occur in large quantities. They look like small white threads about a quarter of an inch long. The eggs of the threadworm are to be found nearly everywhere, even in the soil, and they are spread by flies among other things. The child takes the eggs in through his mouth, and they hatch in the intestines. The larvae then migrate to the rectum. At night the females wriggle out through the anus to lay their eggs and cause severe itching, especially in the evening and at night. Naturally enough, the child scratches the place, and so gets the tiny eggs under his nails. If he then sticks his fingers in his mouth the whole cycle will recommence. Most children and adults have no other trouble from their worms.

Treatment

- There are various effective remedies for threadworms. If one member of the family is suffering from them the whole family must be treated, otherwise the treatment will be ineffective. It is sometimes necessary to take two doses with an interval of several weeks between them.
- Put the child to bed in well-fitting pants or a one-piece sleeping suit to prevent him scratching his buttocks.
- Keep his nails short.
- Everybody in the family must be extra careful over hygiene and must wash their hands frequently, especially before meals and after visiting the WC.

Roundworms

The roundworm is much more unpleasant than the threadworm, but is fortunately very rare in Britain.

The larvae enter our bodies via raw greens and infected soil. They burrow through the wall of the intestines and are carried by the blood to the lungs. From there they are coughed up and are then swallowed into the stomach and intestines, where they develop. The adult worms are 3–8 inches (75–200mm) long and look like white earthworms. When only one worm is present – as is usually the case – there are usually no symptoms; when a child has a number of roundworms, however, he can suffer from abdominal pain and loss of appetite. The worm is discovered only if it is passed in the faeces, or when it is brought up when the child coughs or vomits.

Treatment

Ask the doctor for his advice. There are effective medicines for dealing with these unwelcome parasites.

Tapeworms

The tapeworm lodges itself in the small intestine and the white, ribbon-like segments are evacuated from the bowels. There are different kinds of tapeworm, taken in by eating underdone beef or pork or fish or, in children, by direct contact with infected dogs or cats.

The symptoms are emaciation and sometimes abdominal pain.

Nowadays the tapeworm is very rare in Britain.

Treatment

Effective medicines can be obtained on the doctor's prescription.

I can't get to sleep . . .

Symptoms of nervousness

Most children have behavioural problems at some time or other. Generally this is to do with their natural disposition and development, but sometimes they are reacting to some form of stress. Even happy events such as Christmas and birthdays can make sensitive children anxious and uncertain.

Many parents aggravate the problems arising from their offspring's difficult behaviour. A child that will not eat or sleep, or that wets the bed, creates a lot of work but is in no way unusual. The less fuss is made about the problem the sooner will it be over.

However, if the trouble does not disappear, or if it is really worrying you and the child, you must ask the doctor for advice. He will be able to refer you to a specialist if his own suggestions fail to help.

Sleep problems

Each child has its own particular sleep requirements. Most infants start sleeping through the night after their first few months, others still keep waking up during the night, and others find it hard to go to sleep. Sleep problems have all sorts of causes. A child who has been hard at play just before going to bed can find it difficult to settle down to sleep. A youngster of three or four can find it really hard to wind down in the evening. At this age a child really needs his parents' company; so, if he has been at nursery school, let him stay up a bit longer, and arrange for him to have a midday nap to compensate.

Sleep can also be disturbed by a stuffed-up nose during a cold, by threadworms and by teething difficulties.

Difficulty in falling asleep or other sleep problems can also be a sign that a child feels insecure, or that too much is being required of him in some way, or simply that he wants more attention.

Often it is enough to understand the cause and to accept the situation. Mostly it is adults, not children, who feel the worse for wear after a broken night's sleep.

Loss of appetite

If a child is healthy in other respects there is no need to worry if he goes off his food for a short time. Do not pay too much attention to the amount he eats, but give him increasingly small portions and cut out snacks between meals as these reduce the appetite.

The problem arises, as often as not, because a child does not fancy what you have served up, or because he has a difference of opinion with you over how to eat it. The more you try to make him conform to rules and regulations, the more he will try to make his presence felt at mealtimes.

Comforters

Most children when they are tired or miserable look for something to comfort them.

Some youngsters suck their thumbs or a dummy or hug a teddybear, others rub their cheeks with a piece of cloth, tug on a strand of hair or rock themselves backward and forward.

This is quite normal, but when a child takes refuge in comforters instead of playing with his friends or his parents, something could be wrong.

The child might need extra reassurance because of the arrival of a new brother or sister; unreasonable expectations or demands from the parents; or too much time spent at the crèche or nursery. Try to find the cause, and pay the child a little extra attention.

Tics

A tic is an involuntary contraction of certain groups of muscles. For example, a child may keep blinking his eyes, grimacing or coughing. These movements may have been caused by a sore throat or eye irritation originally, but habits such as blinking and coughing will continue long after the cause has disappeared. A tic can also arise because the child is unconsciously imitating somebody. This is especially likely to happen during a period when he is nervous or unsettled because excessive demands are being placed on him, or because he is under stress. If you try to ignore the tic as much as possible, it will usually stop spontaneously.

Umbilical colic

Pure nervousness will often give children 'stomach-ache', the so-called umbilical colic. Exciting events such as Christmas and birthdays are quite likely to cause it. Usually the pain is not too bad, but it can be quite severe.

However, do not ignore the symptoms; they *could* be warning signs of a serious illness. If the umbilical colic fails to run its normal course, if the child has a rise in temperature or looks worn out, there is obviously some physical cause.

Bed-wetting

When a child is 2–3 years old, he will usually ask to be put on the pot during the day or will sit on it of his own accord. It will then be another six months or so before he is dry at night. A child cannot keep his urination under control until certain reflex paths to the brain are fully developed. This happens at different times in different children, and sometimes it may be delayed. 5–10 per cent of all five-year-olds wet their beds, and some also find it difficult to stay dry during the day. These are nearly always very lively children who do not think of going to the lavatory until the first drops start wetting their pants. What we mean by bed-wetters are girls of 4 years and over and boys of 5 years and over who are still not dry at night. Bed-wetting is often inherited: 70–80 per cent of all children who wet their beds have a father or mother who did the same. Bed-wetters often sleep extremely deeply; it is almost impossible to wake them.

Sometimes a child wets his bed because he wants to feel small and be 'fussed over'. Perhaps a baby brother or sister has come along, or his parents have separated. Of course, some disease or a defect in the urinary passages may be the cause, but in that case the symptoms will occur during the day as well as during the night. If your child is a bed-wetter, consult the health centre, the clinic, or your doctor. They will carry out a physical examination and take a urine sample to see whether some infection is to blame. They will also look at the child's family background, his physical and mental maturity, any mental problems etc.

If no obvious defects are found, the doctor may prescribe tablets to make the sleep lighter, or a special alarm to rouse the child as soon as the first few drops of urine are passed.

If there is reason to suppose that mental problems are at the root of the bed-wetting your doctor will probably refer you to a specialist. However, nearly all bed-wetters grow out of the habit without special treatment if they are not scolded or smacked but treated with patience. Nevertheless, from a psychological point of view, the sooner the child is free from the problem the better for all concerned.

Encopresis

Between the ages of one and three years old, most children become capable of saying when they need to pass a stool. However, there are some who are still not keen on sitting on the pot, and behave as if they were still in nappies.

This may be no more than a half-conscious protest against strict and unsympathetic toilet training, but can point in some cases to a deeper disturbance, which is often associated with psycho-somatic symptoms. The doctor's advice should be sought in good time.

Stuttering

It is perfectly normal for toddlers to stammer or to hesitate between one word and the next, but it is less normal when stuttering becomes permanent. Try not to correct a child more than is necessary when he starts to repeat syllables or stops to think of a word. Listen to *what* he is saying, not to *how* he is saying it. He ought to be able to feel that you like hearing him talk, so try not to show irritation or impatience. Sometimes a child who used to talk well suddenly develops a stutter. Often other symptoms will be present which indicate that he feels unwanted.

The stuttering usually ceases of its own accord, but some children remain inhibited and diffident about speaking. Their lack of self-assurance makes it hard for them to stop stuttering, and in that case medical advice is required.

There is seldom much point in trying to treat stuttering before a child is 5–6 years old and able to co-operate in the cure.

Breath-holding

Children between one and four years old will sometimes hold their breath when crying. What happens is this: a child loses his temper because he cannot get his own way, he begins to cry loudly, tenses his body, and carries on until he turns blue. Sometimes he can faint (for 5–10 seconds), after which he starts breathing normally again.

An attack of this kind can make you so anxious that you give in to the child next time, but try to keep calm and find some way of distracting his attention. Some children have these attacks so often that they may need to be given medicine for a little while to stop them.

Growing pains

'Growing pains' are mainly encountered in lively children between the ages of 4 and 7 years, but can also occur earlier or later. A child will complain on going to bed at night of pain in the lower legs – often in the shins. At other times the pain can be in the calf muscles, which are hard and tense. There is still no satisfactory explanation of growing pains.

Massaging the calves and giving a junior aspirin tablet are frequently very helpful. Children who are subject to growing pains suffer more from them at some periods than at others. When the pain is so severe that the family's rest is disturbed at night, junior aspirin may be given several evenings running during the difficult periods.

Migraine

Migraine, in the form of recurrent attacks of vomiting, may begin as early as six months of age. It is usually hereditary. An attack of migraine can have a mental cause, but may also be triggered by strong light, by the flickering of a TV screen, by hunger, fatigue and train-sickness. The migraine begins because blood-vessels in the brain contract strongly. When the contraction lessens and the blood-vessels dilate, the headache starts – often on one side, and accompanied by nausea and vomiting. Small children find it difficult to describe just where they feel the pain. However, the general symptoms are usually irritability, a throbbing head and sometimes vomiting. Older children can sense when an attack is coming on, but usually do not know what to do to prevent it. They complain of a severe headache – often the whole head aches – and they feel dizzy and sick. If you think your child has migraine you must consult the doctor to find out what brings on the attacks, and to obtain any medicine he may wish to prescribe. Children often benefit from simple remedies, and there are also very effective drugs for preventing or relieving the attacks in the more severe cases.

Headache due to stress

Headache due to stress will occur when children are still very young. It is usually experienced over the crown and causes tension in the neck muscles; this tension causes another headache, and a vicious circle that is hard to break is set up. Try to relieve the tension in the neck muscles by massage or relaxation exercises.

Sources of help

The family physician or the school doctor will always advise you. It is possible that they will refer you and your child to a specialist psychiatrist for examination and possible treatment.

The commonest infectious diseases of childhood

Disease	Cause	Incubation period	Symptoms
whooping-cough	bacterium	5–14 days	cold and cough; after 3 weeks cough becomes louder and often crowing, vomiting occurs
measles	a virus	10–12 days	cold, dry cough, high temperature, red and watery eyes; the rash starts on the third or fourth day behind the ears
mumps	a virus	17–21 days	high temperature, swollen parotid glands
German measles	a virus	17–18 days	cold, sore throat, slight temperature rise, painful joints; the rash starts on the second or fourth day; swollen, sometimes painful, lymph glands, especially in the neck
scarlet fever	bacteria (haemolytic streptococci)	2–5 days	high temperature, sore throat, swollen tonsils; the rash starts after one day, especially around the armpits and the groin; strawberry tongue; the skin peels after 2–4 weeks
roseola	a virus	7–14 days	a high temperature for 3 to 4 days; perhaps slight symptoms of a cold; a pink rash when the fever disappears
chicken-pox	a virus	14–16 days	a high temperature; after a few hours the rash becomes vesicular (it looks like small blisters)

Treatment	Complications	Immunity	Prevention
fresh air; raise the head of the bed; perhaps antibiotics	rare nowadays; bronchitis, pneumonia	lifelong	inoculation at the age of 3–6 months
rest in bed as long as the fever lasts; perhaps something to bring the temperature down	earache, pneumonia, encephalitis	lifelong	inoculation between 12 and 24 months
rest in bed as long as the fever lasts	meningitis, orchitis (inflammation of the testicles)	lifelong	none
rest in bed as long as the fever lasts	foetal damage in pregnant women during the first three months	lifelong	inoculation for girls between the ages of 10 and 14 years
penicillin; rest in bed as long as the fever lasts	nephritis	can recur	none
rest in bed as long as the fever lasts; perhaps something to bring the temperature down	perhaps infantile convulsions	probably lifelong	none
rest in bed as long as the fever lasts; an ointment for the irritation	rare	lifelong	none

Measles (rubeola)

Measles was once the commonest disease of childhood, and most children caught it before they were old enough to start school. Nowadays, inoculation is available.

Infectiousness

Measles is a very infectious disease, and a child will be readily infected by the virus if he is occupying the same room as a measles patient. The spread of the disease is via droplets sprayed into the air as the patient coughs or breathes. On the other hand, a fit person who is nursing the patient does not become a carrier. Measles is infectious 2−4 days before the rash appears. When you know that your child is suffering from the disease, keep him home from school for nine days after the infection has taken place. This will stop the spread of the disease; a child with measles is infectious until the rash begins to fade after about a week.

One attack of measles usually confers immunity for life. Babies enjoy an immunity to measles for the first 6 months of life if their mothers have had the disease.

The course of the illness

From the moment a child is infected it takes from 10−12 days (usually 11 days) for the symptoms to appear. The first symptoms resemble those of a common cold − there is a discharge from the nose, a hoarse, harsh cough and fever. The eyes are red and inflamed and sensitive to light. For the first two days the temperature is 100·5−102·5°F (38−39°C); it then falls for a few days before rising to as much as 104°F (40°C). At this stage the rash appears. After 2−4 days the temperature falls once more. In small children the catarrhal symptoms are often quite marked in the first few days.

The initial spots are very small (between 2−6mm), scarlet-coloured, irregular and slightly raised. They coalesce and become reddish blue. The rash starts on the throat and behind the ears, then spreads to the cheeks and the rest of the body. It causes irritation.

Several days before the rash appears, small red spots, each of which has a white speck in the middle, can be seen on the cheeks inside the mouth.

Treatment

- The child will usually prefer to stay in bed as long as he is feverish. If the high temperature is making him very ill, give him something like junior aspirin to bring it down.

The rash in measles starts as small, scarlet spots. These later merge and become reddish-brown.

A typical measles temperature chart

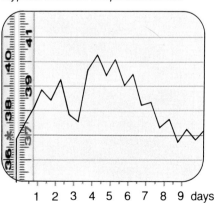

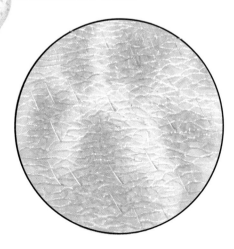

Incubation period: 10–12 days.

Symptoms: Begins like a cold with runny nose, dry cough and a rise in temperature. The eyes become red and sore. The rash appears on the third or fourth day and starts on the neck.

Treatment: Rest in bed as long as the fever lasts. Perhaps something to bring the temperature down.

Complications: Earache, pneumonia, meningitis. In certain complications antibiotics are given.

Notify the doctor if the fever lasts longer than 4 days from the appearance of the rash, or if there are signs of complications.

Inoculation: Measles inoculations are given from 14 months onward. Infected children between 6 months and 2 years old, like chronically ill children who have not been inoculated, should be given gamma globulin if they have been exposed to measles. This substance offers short-term protection.

Return to nursery or school: 7 days after the rash appears, provided the temperature has been normal for at least 3 days and the child seems fit and well again.

- Cough medicines seldom ease the cough.
- The chemist will be able to recommend an ointment to soothe the itching. Ordinary talcum powder can also help.
- The sore eyes can be bathed with water. Dim the bedroom light for the child; a bright light will irritate his eyes even more.

Complications

Measles is no longer a dangerous disease, but you must check to see whether or not the temperature goes down. When a child still has a high temperature 3–4 days after the rash appears, you must call the doctor. There could be complications such as earache or pneumonia. You must also contact the doctor if the child has inflammation of the ear or difficulty in breathing.

Another possibility is meningitis, in which case the fever rises again, the child becomes drowsy and sometimes vomits or suffers from convulsions.

Inoculation

When a child is between 12 and 24 months old he can be inoculated against measles. A weakened form of the measles virus is injected. The inoculation offers long-term immunity.

Approximately one-third of the children who are inoculated have a slight rise in temperature and come out in pale spots which quickly disappear. This takes place after about a week, but the child is not infectious. Children who are oversensitive to eggs can react to the vaccine; in this case special precautions have to be taken.

Children between the ages of 6 months and 2 years can be very ill with measles. If you have a child of this age who is infected he ought to be given gamma globulin within 5 days of the infection. In this way the disease can be prevented or be reduced in severity. Gamma globulin is available only through the doctor.

Measles and pregnancy

As far as is known, measles is not dangerous to the unborn child. Nevertheless, a pregnant woman who has never had measles should not unnecessarily expose herself to infection during the first months of pregnancy.

German measles (rubella)

Incubation period: 2–3 weeks, usually 17–18 days.

Symptoms: The symptoms of a light cold, a runny nose, slight temperature rise, sometimes joint pain. Rash after 2–3 days. Swollen, sensitive lymphatic glands, especially in the neck.

Notifying the doctor: Pregnant women who have never had German measles, or have not been properly inoculated, must get in touch with their doctors if they suspect that they could have been infected.

Treatment: No special treatment required.

Inoculation: Girls who have not had German measles can be inoculated when they are 10–14 years old.

Return to the nursery or to school: When the rash has disappeared and the child seems fit and well again.

German measles is a virus disease like measles, but the illness does not last so long and it is not so contagious. The disease is not dangerous to children. It usually attacks toddlers and tends to occur in epidemics.

Infectiousness

A child can be infected with German measles both by direct contact and by droplets which the German measles patient spreads around him when he coughs or sneezes. A person is infectious from 2–3 days before the disease breaks out until a few days after the disappearance of the rash. One attack of German measles gives lifelong immunity.

The course of the illness

The initial symptoms resemble those of a normal light cold: a runny nose, a mild sore throat and a temperature of approximately 100·5°F (38°C). Sometimes the child suffers from a headache. Older children in particular will often have pains in the joints for several days. Usually these symptoms are so mild that they go unnoticed.

After a few days the rash appears. Small spots are found first on the face and then on the trunk, sometimes on the arms and legs as well. The spots are pale pink and flat, and are not so closely crowded as in measles. On the face they can overlap, so that the cheeks look weather-beaten. Sometimes the rash is so slight as to be hardly visible.

The lymphatic glands are usually swollen and sensitive, especially in the neck, but also under the armpits and in the groin. When the rash fades 2–3 days later the fever abates too, and the symptoms of a head cold disappear.

Treatment

Keep the child indoors but let him get up if he wants to, provided he keeps quiet.

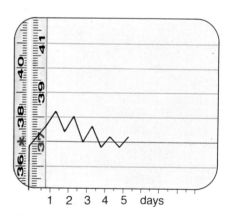

A typical German measles temperature chart.

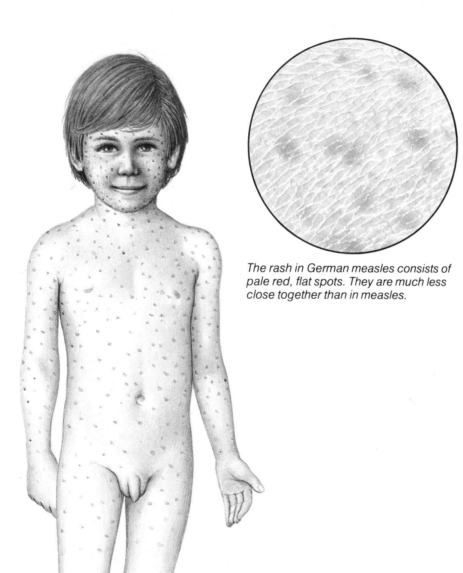

The rash in German measles consists of pale red, flat spots. They are much less close together than in measles.

Complications

German measles is not often accompanied by complications. When you are not sure whether the case is one of German measles, let a doctor or nurse make the diagnosis, especially if the patient is a girl.

The reason why German measles is not to be taken lightly is the potential danger it represents for an unborn child during the first three months of pregnancy. If you are pregnant and think you have been infected with the disease, but are not sure that you are immune to it, get in touch with your doctor or with the hospital, so that they can keep you under observation. A blood-test can be taken to determine if you are already immune: you may, for instance, have had a mild form of German measles previously, or have been inoculated when too young to remember. Two blood-tests a few weeks apart will show whether you are in fact suffering from the disease.

Inoculation

Since German measles is a fairly harmless disease without complications, there is no need to inoculate small children against it. However, when girls are between 10 and 14 years old and it is not absolutely certain that they have had the disease, inoculation is wise since it will forestall problems in any future pregnancies.

Chickenpox

Incubation period: 2–3 weeks. Usually 14–16 days.

Symptoms: Often begins with fever, 100·5–102·5°F (38–39°C). The rash appears simultaneously as red spots which fill with fluid in the course of a few hours.

Treatment: Rest in bed if necessary. Ointment, calamine lotion or talc for the itching. Keep the nails short and clean.

Complications: If the child manages to scratch the vesicles open they can become infected with putrefactive bacteria.

Inoculation: There is no vaccine for chickenpox.

Return to the nursery or to school: When the vesicles have dried up (usually after 7–14 days).

Chickenpox is a relatively mild childhood disease that most children catch. The disease is caused by a virus – the same virus that can cause shingles in adults.

Infectiousness

Next to measles, chickenpox is the most infectious of all childhood diseases. The infection is conveyed by direct contact or by droplets coughed into the atmosphere. A child is infectious from the day before the rash appears until the day the vesicles dry up, usually 5–7 days later. The risk of infecting others is greatest in the first few days.

Babies are generally immune to chickenpox in their first six months if their mothers have had the disease.

It is possible for adults to go down with shingles when infected by a child with chickenpox, and children can catch chickenpox from adults with shingles.

The course of the illness

The incubation period varies from 2–3 weeks, usually 14–16 days. Chickenpox often starts with a temperature of 100·5–102·5°F (38–39°C), which persists for a couple of days. Small children usually have only a slight rise in temperature or none at all. The rash appears almost at the same time as the fever. First it takes the form of tiny red pimples about 2 mm in diameter. Within a few hours the pimples change into oval vesicles which resemble drops of water, and which itch. When the time comes for the vesicles to break they dry to form dark crusts, which fall off after 10–14 days.

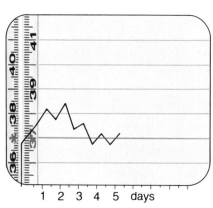

A typical Chickenpox temperature chart.

In chickenpox the rash usually starts on the trunk, spreading to the face, behind the ears, the scalp, and the arms and legs. It initially takes the form of small red pimples which quickly change to blisters. The blisters break easily and dry to become covered in crusts.

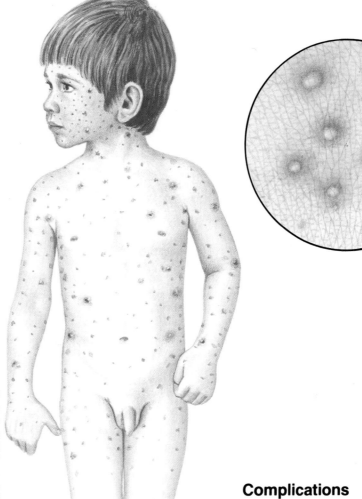

The rash spreads over the whole body, appearing first on the trunk, then on the face, behind the ears, on the scalp, and on the arms and legs. The vesicles can also affect the mucous membrane of the mouth, and occur on the ears and genitals. There is no rash on the palms of the hands or the soles of the feet.

For 4–5 days the rash can continue to break out and run through all the stages of development and healing: red pimples, vesicles and crusts.

In small children chickenpox can be confused with a sort of nettle rash known as strophulus. The difference is that in strophulus the blisters all appear at once, and not on the scalp or in the mouth.

Treatment

- The child need not stay in bed unless he feels like it.
- The irritation can be allayed with calamine lotion, talc or ointment.
- Keep the nails short and clean to minimize the risk of infection.
- Do not give the child a bath before the crusts are dry.
- Do not let him come in contact with other children before the crusts are dry. However, he may go out of doors as soon as he seems well enough.
- If the itching is very intense and the child finds it difficult to sleep, ask the doctor for suitable medicine.
- Children who are still in nappies should wear them as little as possible.

Complications

Chickenpox does not usually involve complications. If a child tears the vesicles open with his nails they can become infected by pus-forming bacteria and leave behind small pits in the skin. Also, when you wash the child, take special care not to rub off any of the crusts – a crust that comes away too soon leaves a permanent scar.

Inoculation

There is no vaccine for chickenpox. In special cases an infected child will be given gamma globulin so that the disease runs a milder course.

Scarlet fever

Incubation period: 2–4 days.

Symptoms: High temperature, sore throat, enlarged and inflamed tonsils. After about a day red spots appear, first under the armpits and in the groin. Red cheeks and pale skin round the mouth. Red tongue. Possible peeling of the skin after 2–4 weeks, especially from the palms of the hands, the soles of the feet, fingers and toes.

Treatment: Penicillin. Bed rest according to individual needs.

Complications: Unusual when penicillin is given, but occasionally nephritis.

Notify the doctor if you think your child has scarlet fever.

Vaccination: None.

Return to the nursery or to school: after one week if the child is well again and has been given antibiotics.

Scarlet fever is an infection of the throat which can occur at any time of life. However, young school-children are those most at risk. Unweaned infants seldom catch it.

Scarlet fever used to be greatly feared because of its complications and patients were isolated in a fever hospital. For some unknown reason the disease has become milder, and is less common nowadays. What is more, thanks to penicillin, the risk of complications has been greatly reduced.

Infectiousness

Scarlet fever is caused by bacteria, the type called streptococci. The bacteria spread very quickly and are carried by such things as toys, towels and bedding. Without treatment a person is infectious from the moment the disease is contracted to the day that desquamation (peeling) is over. People can also be carriers without being ill themselves. Scarlet fever can be caught several times.

Course

The incubation period is 2–5 days. The initial symptoms are those of a sore throat: the child has a fever, sometimes rising to 104°F (40°C), his throat feels sore, his tonsils become swollen and inflamed and are sometimes covered in white spots. Other symptoms are headache and vomiting.

One to three days later the rash appears in the form of closely crowded red spots the size of a pin-head. Later the spots tend to run together. They can be slightly raised, so that the skin feels rough, like gooseflesh. The rash begins under the armpits and in the groin and then spreads over the abdomen, the right and left side, the back, along the arms and legs and on the neck. Sometimes the tiny spots are scarcely visible.

The face is usually free from the rash but the cheeks are red and the part round the mouth is pale. The tongue is coated for the first few days, and then turns bright red because it is studded with small red spots. This is traditionally known as a 'strawberry tongue'.

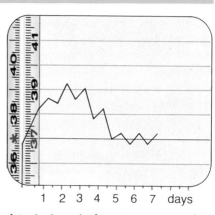

A typical scarlet fever temperature chart.

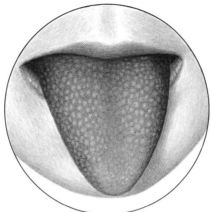

The papillae of the tongue become red and swollen to give the so-called 'strawberry tongue'.

In 2–4 weeks the skin starts to peel, especially on the fingers and toes, on the palms and on the soles of the feet.

The rash in scarlet fever consists of closely crowded red spots the size of a pin-head, slightly raised above the skin. They start in front of the armpits and in the groin and then spread over the abdomen and back and along the arms and legs.

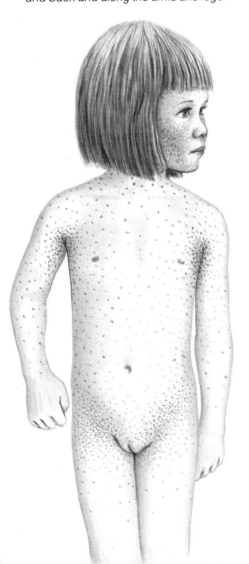

Without treatment the temperature falls slowly and is normal once more in about a week. The rash has usually also faded by then. Two to four weeks after the start of the disease the skin starts to peel, especially from the palms of the hands, the soles of the feet and the fingers and toes. Peeling is usually over in a week. In mild cases of scarlet fever peeling can be the only sign that the child has really had the disease. If penicillin is given early there is usually no peeling.

Treatment

- Sometimes it is difficult to determine whether or not a child has scarlet fever, since measles, German measles and roseola have the same sort of rash. Generally speaking, the clinical picture as a whole will decide. If you suspect that your child has scarlet fever, consult the doctor; if in doubt he can take a throat swab to confirm the presence of streptococci.
- Scarlet fever is treated with penicillin. This shortens the duration of the disease and reduces the danger of complications.
- Let the child stay in bed as long as he feels like it.
- Keep the child at home from school until he is completely well again (usually in 7–10 days).

Complications

Nowadays scarlet fever is no longer a serious disease and usually there are no complications. Occasionally nephritis occurs (mostly in a mild form), so the doctor may wish to have urine samples.

Inoculation

There is no vaccine for scarlet fever.

Mumps

Mumps is not so common in children as are measles or chickenpox, but more than half of all children go down with it before reaching school age. The disease chiefly affects children between the ages of 5 and 9 years, and the younger the child the milder the disease. Babies under 6 months old do not catch mumps if their mothers have had the disease.

In mumps the parotid glands – which lie in front of the ear and in the lower angle of the jaw – swell up.

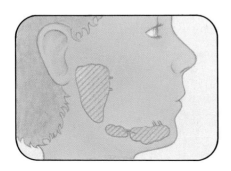

Infectiousness

Mumps is a virus disease, and the infection is by direct contact. The virus perishes very quickly in the air, so the disease cannot be carried by bedding or playthings.

One attack of mumps usually confers lifelong immunity from the disease, but occasionally someone catches it again.

The course of the illness

The incubation period can vary a little, but usually it is between 17 and 21 days. The first symptom is a temperature of 100·5–102·5°F (38–39°C) and sometimes higher. After a few days the glands in front of and under the ears swell. When the swelling is very pronounced it can even force the ear-lobes up. Often when the fever comes the swelling is on one side, and the other side of the face swells only after some days, when the temperature suddenly rises again after falling. However, it is possible for the swelling to be one-sided from start to finish. In some cases the pancreas becomes inflamed too, and as a result there is severe abdominal pain. In the absence of complications, mumps is usually over in about a week.

Treatment

- Small children are usually not very ill. If a child runs a high temperature and is feeling wretched, you may give him something to bring it down, for example junior aspirin.

Incubation period: 17–21 days.

Symptoms: High temperature, swollen parotid glands.

Treatment: Rest in bed as long as the temperature is high and the child is suffering. Give something to bring the temperature down if necessary (aspirin).

Complications: A fairly mild attack of meningitis can occur at any age. Inflammation of the testicles (orchitis) is possible in boys after puberty.

Notify the doctor: If your child seems to have a serious complication.

Inoculation: None.

Return to the nursery or to school: When the swelling has gone down and the temperature has been normal for 3 or 4 days (usually after 10–14 days).

- Children over the age of 5 or 6 years must be kept in quiet surroundings until they have been free from fever for several days. This reduces the chance of meningitis.
- Give liquid food if the child has difficulty in chewing and swallowing.
- Do not give him anything sour to eat, as this will stimulate the salivary glands.
- Call the doctor if you think meningitis or inflammation of the testicles has occurred as a complication.

seldom leads to sterility. However, the pain can be very trying.

A mild form of meningitis is a very frequent complication in both children and adults. The first signs are nausea, headache and feverishness when the mumps seems to be over. After several days there is a stiff neck. Meningitis in mumps is usually benign and is over within a week. Occasionally the symptoms are so severe that the child will have to be admitted to hospital. Impaired hearing or deafness often result in such cases.

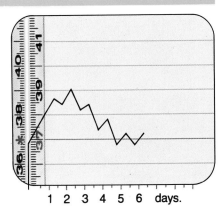

A typical mumps temperature chart.

Complications

Youngsters who have passed the age of puberty can suffer from inflammation of the testicles when they catch mumps. This happens when they have been free from fever for several days. The fever then returns, with the temperature rising to 104°F (40°C), and the testicles become sensitive and enlarged. The inflammation lasts 1–2 weeks as a general rule, and

Whooping-cough

Incubation period: 7–14 days, usually 7 days.

Symptoms: Begins as a cold with a runny nose and cough. Little or no rise in temperature. For 3 weeks the cough grows worse and the child 'whoops' and vomits, especially at night. The cough then moderates for 2–3 weeks.

Complications: Bronchitis, pneumonia.

Treatment: Fresh air. Possibly antibiotics.

Notifying the doctor: Small children need to be seen by a doctor when the disease looks serious.

Inoculation: Babies are inoculated 3 times against whooping-cough.

Return to the nursery or to school: 6 weeks after the start of the cough (approx. 4 weeks after the whooping begins).

Infectiousness

Whooping-cough is a bacterial infection, and the germs are carried by the droplets coughed by an infected child. An individual is infectious from the start of the cough until 4 or 5 weeks later. Infectiousness is greatest in the beginning of the disease.

Unweaned infants have no inborn immunity, even when their mothers have had whooping-cough. Therefore you should take great care to keep a baby away from infection. Once you have had whooping-cough you have long-term but not lifelong immunity, so grandparents should not be exposed to infection.

The course of the illness

The incubation period for whooping-cough is 7–14 days, usually 7 days. The disease starts with a runny nose and a cough, exactly like a common cold. The temperature is either normal or slightly raised. In the beginning it is rather difficult to say whether the case is really one of whooping-cough. This stage can last for a few weeks. After that the cough grows worse and the child suffers from severe paroxysms of coughing, especially during the night and at mealtimes, and sometimes finds it hard to draw breath; he then starts to whoop. His face turns purple with the effort to inhale, and he makes a crowing sound while breathing in. A quantity of sticky, ropy mucus is brought up into the mouth, and is frequently expectorated by the child. These paroxysms usually cease within 2–3 weeks.

Treatment

- When the child is more than 3 or 4 years old and is otherwise healthy, and the whooping-cough does not appear to be particularly serious, there is no need to call the doctor.
- When the child is under the age of three years or when he is run down because of some other illness, it will be necessary for him to have medical attention. Modern medicines are available which can help to shorten the course of the disease and to alleviate the coughing attacks. Ordinary cough linctuses are no use. Babies sometimes have to be admitted to hospital for a few weeks until the worst is over.
- Often you will have to stay beside the bed of a small child right through the night. If he is supported in a half-sitting position he will find it easier to breathe during the attacks of coughing.
- It is good for the child to be out of doors in the fresh air. The paroxysms are then often less severe.

- Eating is usually a great problem because it is liable to provoke a fit of coughing, and the child may even vomit. The best plan is to try to get him to eat something shortly after one of his coughing fits, when he is enjoying a respite. Give him small portions of food that is easy to chew and digest, and allow him to eat fairly often.
- Keep the child away from school as long as he is infectious – i.e., for 4–6 weeks. The period of infectiousness can be shortened by antibiotics.

Fresh air out of doors will do your child good if he has whooping-cough. The attacks of coughing are then often less severe. But make sure he does not play with other children, as he may pass the disease on to them.

Complications

Sometimes a child contracts a respiratory infection as a complication. In this event antibiotics are very effective. The cough can be very persistent, and readily recurs during the first few months after whooping-cough.

Inoculation

Babies are inoculated against whooping-cough at 3, 5–6 and 9–11 months. The protection wears off later when they go to school. Children who are not robust will benefit from antibiotics when they catch whooping-cough, but these must be given before the whooping stage is reached.

Other infectious diseases

Roseola

Roseola is a virus disease that occurs in children between the ages of six months and three years, and sometimes in children a little older. Immunity is probably lifelong.

Infectiousness

Roseola is infectious by direct contact. However, it is not a particularly infectious disease, and a child can suffer from it without passing it on to his brothers or sisters. When the disease occurs in a mild form and without a rash, it is sometimes difficult to diagnose.

Infectiousness ceases when the temperature rises.

The course of the illness

The incubation period varies, but is usually within the region of 14 days. The child suddenly gets a high temperature of 102·5−104°F (39−40°C) without other symptoms. The fever lasts 3 or 4 days. In spite of being feverish the child seems to feel fairly well: he eats and sleeps normally, but may be a little more irritable and hard to please than at other times. At the moment the temperature returns to normal on the third or fourth day he breaks out in a rash in the form of pale red spots which spread over the whole body and usually fade in a few days. Sometimes they fade so quickly that they go unnoticed. As soon as the rash has disappeared the illness is over.

Treatment

- Rest in bed is seldom necessary. The bedroom should be cool, and there should not be too many covers on the bed.
- Because the temperature rises very quickly, some children suffer from convulsions (see page 60).
- Keep the child indoors as long as he is feverish.

Complications

The doctor must be notified if the child has convulsions. Otherwise the disease is not dangerous.

Inoculation

There is no roseola vaccine.

Glandular fever

Glandular fever is a virus disease that affects schoolchildren in particular. Infection is by direct contact.

The course of the illness

The symptoms are similar to those of tonsillitis: a rise in temperature and inflamed, swollen tonsils. However, the lymphatic glands in the angle of the jaw and in the neck are much more swollen than they are in tonsillitis. Even the glands in the groin and armpits often become enlarged. A rash can occur, mostly on the abdomen. In about a week the temperature falls, but the remaining symptoms − low fever, swollen glands and a sore throat − can persist for weeks, so that the child stays tired and listless.

Treatment

- The illness usually goes away without special treatment. Antibiotics are of no assistance in this case.
- Keep the child in restful surroundings as long as his temperature is high.

Complications

Complications do not usually occur during childhood years, but sometimes there is a bacterial infection in the throat as well. In this case, antibiotics will in fact prove helpful.

A typical roseola temperature chart.

Impetigo

Impetigo is caused by an infection of the skin caused by putrefactive bacteria. The disease can occur at any time of life. Sometimes a minor epidemic occurs at schools or other places where children collect. The disease is often accompanied by a cold.

Infectiousness

Impetigo is infectious. The infection is conveyed by direct contact with someone who is infectious, also by hand towels or flannels. Putrefactive bacteria penetrate the skin where the surface is irritated or chafed. Impetigo is infectious as long as the sores have not healed, and the child must not return to school as long as the scabs are present. One attack of impetigo does not confer automatic immunity from a second attack.

The course of the illness

Signs of the disease appear 2–5 days after infection, generally speaking. The rash takes the form of small pustules filled with yellow liquid or sticky substance. Often it starts around the mouth or nose but can also occur on other parts of the body, especially on places already affected by boils or patches of eczema. The pustules become covered in honey-yellow scabs.

Treatment

- One quite effective if somewhat old-fashioned treatment is to wash the sores with a cooking-salt solution (1 large teaspoonful of cooking salt in 17½ fluid ounces (½ litre) of boiled water). Rub the incrustations away and apply a bactericidal or zinc ointment. Treat the pustules every day until they have disappeared.

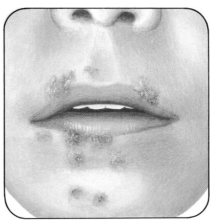

The sticky, yellow rash often commences round the mouth or nose.

- Consult the doctor if a child is infected on many places or if his throat becomes inflamed. In this case, he may need antibiotics.

Complications

If neglected, impetigo can result in nephritis.

Cold sore
(herpes simplex)

Most people, both children and adults, are carriers of a virus known as herpes simplex. Usually there are no signs of its presence, but sometimes this virus causes an infection of the mouth, especially when some other infection is active.

Symptoms

Yellow-white blisters which break out on the palate, on the inside of the cheeks, on the gums and on the tongue, are typical symptoms. The gums are swollen and inflamed. The child has a high temperature, feels ill and has bad breath. It is often very difficult for him to eat solid food, and he may even avoid drinking because it hurts his mouth. After a few days similar vesicles and pustules come up on the lips.

Treatment

- Herpes in the mouth clears up in about a week. There is no special treatment for it.
- The child may be given junior aspirin for the soreness in his mouth.
- Give liquid food; something that is cold and not sour. However, liquid food too can be difficult to manage if the infection is very severe. A drinking straw can ease the situation.
- Let the child rinse his mouth freely.

Meningitis

Meningitis is the general name for symptoms caused by an irritation of the meninges – i.e., the membranes surrounding the brain. A distinction is drawn between two kinds of meningitis: *bacterial meningitis*, caused by bacteria and occurring not only as a complication in certain infections of the respiratory passages but also as a complaint in its own right, and *viral meningitis*, which also occurs as a separate infection or as a complication in other infections – in this case, in other virus infections such as mumps.

Infectiousness

Bacterial meningitis is certainly infectious, but less so than viral meningitis. However, there is a so-called epidemic form.

The course of the illness

In *bacterial meningitis* the temperature rises very quickly. The child suffers from a headache and a stiff neck; he vomits, and is very ill. In babies feverishness and spasms can sometimes be the only symptoms.

In *viral meningitis* the symptoms are similar but less intense. Sometimes there is dizziness. A characteristic of this type of meningitis is that it occurs as a complication when the fever and other symptoms of some virus infection from which a child has been suffering have disappeared for several days. The temperature then suddenly shoots up again.

Ticks can carry a virus that causes meningitis. A child then falls ill within four weeks of being bitten and becomes feverish; sometimes he displays slight symptoms of paralysis.

Treatment

If you suspect that your child has meningitis you must call the doctor or the hospital. In *bacterial meningitis* antibiotics will have to be injected into the bloodstream without delay.

Viral meningitis usually passes off of its own accord. There is no effective medicine for it.

Most children recover from viral meningitis without any permanent damage. Even after a bout of bacterial meningitis, recovery is generally satisfactory if the treatment is begun soon enough. Nevertheless, in babies in particular, certain bacteria can cause permanent damage – e.g., impaired hearing.

Polio

Since the introduction of inoculations for polio the disease has become rare. However, as it does crop up here and there, there is a risk of infection if you have not been properly inoculated (see page 111).

The course of the illness

Polio is caused by a virus, and infects mainly by coughing and by contact with faeces.

Polio often runs a very inconspicuous course. The only symptoms can be a slight fever and perhaps diarrhoea, and the disease can be over in a few days. There are other cases in which the symptoms are a high temperature, a headache and a stiff neck. Symptoms of paralysis are also common, especially in the arms and legs. These symptoms can disappear when the acute phase of the disease is over, but many individuals are permanently paralysed.

Treatment

Polio cases must be isolated for treatment.

Tuberculosis (TB)

Tuberculosis used to be a very common and much dreaded disease, especially in small children and young adults. Thanks to improved hygiene, improved eating habits, vaccination, and an intensive search for the source of the infection, tuberculosis has been almost eradicated. The few cases which do occur involve mainly the children of immigrants and older people.

Infectiousness

Tuberculosis of the lungs is caused by bacteria which are spread as the tubercular patient coughs. The fact that a person has had tuberculosis does not confer lifelong immunity.

The course of the illness

The incubation period is about 6 weeks. In the beginning there are no symptoms other than possibly feverishness for 2–3 weeks. After this the child can become pale and lacking in energy, and loses his appetite. Painful, reddish-blue patches on the fronts of the shins often occur at this stage. In most instances changes (often unobserved) also take place in the lungs.

Treatment

Nowadays there is effective treatment for tuberculosis. Initially, the treatment is given in hospital.

Inoculation

Children in families known to be at risk can be immunized (see page 113).

Skin complaints

Warts

Many children suffer from warts on their hands and from verrucas on the soles of their feet, especially after reaching school age. The warts are caused by a virus that is spread by direct contact or by the floor in the school gymnasium or swimming-pool.

Treatment

- Sooner or later the warts will disappear spontaneously, but this process can be speeded up by rubbing them with a piece of pumice-stone or by filing them with a nail-file. Preparations may also be purchased from the chemists to loosen the warts and to make it easy to pick them out.
- Operations are no longer performed to remove verrucas (even when they are large and painful) from the feet, because it is felt inadvisable to damage the sensitive soles.

Head lice

Nowadays head lice have become fairly rare, but sudden epidemics are still liable to break out in infant schools and day nurseries. When a child contracts head lice he very quickly passes them on to the whole family.

The lice lay eggs at the roots of the hairs, and these can be seen as small white 'nits' glued to the hairs themselves. When the lice move about or bite the scalp the child scratches his head to stop the itching; this produces open wounds which can become infected.

Treatment

Lice are easily treated with a special solution obtainable from the chemist. Follow the directions on the packet precisely. Give everyone in the family the same treatment even if they display no symptoms.

Scabies

Scabies is due to a parasite that is spread by direct contact. The mite burrows into the skin and lays its eggs there, especially between the fingers and toes, or even on the arms and legs and in the navel. The irritation is very intense, especially at night.

Treatment

An ointment or emulsion is smeared over the whole body. Ask the doctor for advice.

Nappy rash

The buttocks of small children readily become red and raw if they are left too long in wet, warm nappies. Sometimes the baby's bottom is covered in small red pimples or the skin is red in patches or wherever the wet nappy has caused irritation.

If the irritation is allowed to persist, fungal infection can occur. The skin then takes on a more vivid red hue and has a flayed appearance.

Treatment

- Nappy rash can be prevented by changing the nappies regularly and by keeping the buttocks as clean and dry as possible.
- When baby is being changed, leave his bottom uncovered for a while and give him a clean, dry nappy to lie on, spread on top of his cot waterproof sheet.
- Use nothing but lukewarm water for washing.
- Smear on a little ointment.
- If the buttocks still remain red ask the local health centre or clinic for advice.

Seborrhoea (cradle cap)

Seborrhoea covers the crown of the head, sometimes in a fairly thick layer of greasy yellow scales. It is not dangerous, but it looks unsightly and is a possible target for infections.

Treatment

A 2 per cent salicylic ointment is rubbed on in the evening and left on over night. Then, in the morning, the baby's head is washed with baby-shampoo or baby-soap and water. After this, the incrustations may be carefully combed out. The treatment is repeated a number of times.

Heat rash

Heat rash occurs mainly on the chest, round the throat and under the arms, either as small pink spots with a yellowish-white head in the centre or as large red patches. It is completely harmless and goes away almost as quickly as it comes.

Rashes due to eating certain foodstuffs

Hypersensitivity to certain foodstuffs or medicines can give rise to a rash (see the section on Allergies, page 54).

Allergy

What is allergy?

Allergy means 'an altered response'. People who are allergic form antibodies, the so-called reagins, when they come in contact with certain – usually quite common – substances in their environment or in their food. These substances are called allergens. When a sufficient number of antibodies have been formed a reaction takes place when fresh contact is made with the allergen. When this happens histamine is released by some of the body cells. The histamine gives the allergic individuals such symptoms as itching, swelling and respiratory difficulties.

A distinction is made between various kinds of allergy:

Bronchial allergy. caused by pollen, dust, fungal spores, animal hair and animal epithelium.

Aliment allergy, caused by certain articles of diet such as eggs, some types of berry, greens, milk, nuts, fish, shellfish and citrus fruit.

Drug allergy, caused by antibiotics such as penicillin and the sulphanilamides, some drugs for epilepsy and even aspirins and aspirin-based products (junior aspirin).

Contact allergy, caused by detergents, creams, formalin (found in certain crease-proof fabrics, in adhesives and in some shampoos). Chrome in plated metals – e.g., in push-buttons and hooks – can also provoke allergic reactions.

Insect allergy, caused by wasp or bee stings. These can cause a very violent reaction.

Predisposition to allergy

Allergy usually depends on inherited factors. If one of the parents is allergic there is a 40 per cent chance that the child will be too. If both parents are allergic the chance is 70 per cent. However, a person can also be allergic without any evident inherited factors.

It is the *tendency* that is inherited, not the allergy itself. Thus a parent who is a victim of hay fever could have a child who reacts with nettle-rash to certain foodstuffs.

It is only after repeated contact with the allergen that the child forms the antibodies which cause the allergy, and suffers from asthma or nettle-rash, for example. If you know that inherited factors are present you should try to stop your child coming into contact unnecessarily with the commonest allergens.

Allergy tests

You must try to find out what your child is allergic to. The doctor will have to help here. Nowadays there are good testing methods, but parents' observations on when the symptoms occur, and which allergens appear to be to blame, still form the most important part of the investigation. A skin test is sometimes performed on children over the age of 4 or 5 years. A small quantity of various allergens is injected into the top layer of skin. When a child is hypersensitive to one of these substances his skin becomes red and swollen after a few minutes.

Aliment allergies are identified by letting the child eat a portion of the suspected food under careful observation. If severe reactions are likely, this must be done in a hospital.

Ridding the house of allergens

Many children are allergic to furred animals. Offending particles can also be shed into the environment by furs, shaggy woollen clothing, wall-to-wall carpeting, pillows, furniture and bedding stuffed with horsehair. Try to keep the house as dust-free as possible. Damp places where moulds could grow must be frequently cleaned, because certain moulds are well-known allergens. A spring-clean can do much to improve matters. For instance, it is a good idea to clear the child's room of oddments and piles of newspapers and magazines.

Foodstuffs as allergens

Milk and cheese are among the commonest allergenic foods eaten by children. Sometimes a child does better on boiled milk and yoghurt. Even certain foods containing milk (bread, for example) can cause reactions. Many children are allergic to eggs – more often to the yolk than to the white – even when they are incorporated in foods such as ice-cream. Children who are liable to eczema do not usually tolerate citrus fruits; however, it may be the oil in the skin of an orange which brings up a rash on a child's hands, and they will be able to drink the juice if someone else squeezes the fruit for them. Allergens such as nuts, fish and shellfish are less usual in children, but the reactions can be very intense when they do occur.

Allergic symptoms

The commonest allergic symptoms in children are eczema, asthma, respiratory allergies (such as hay fever) and nettle-rash (urticaria). The symptoms vary depending on the place where the allergic reaction occurs. If the reaction occurs in the nose the child suffers from the symptoms of a cold; if it occurs in the bronchi he suffers from asthma; in eczema and nettle-rash the reaction takes place in the skin. Some children get diarrhoea or stomach-ache from certain foodstuffs, and allergic shock can follow as a severe reaction to wasp or bee stings.

Eczema

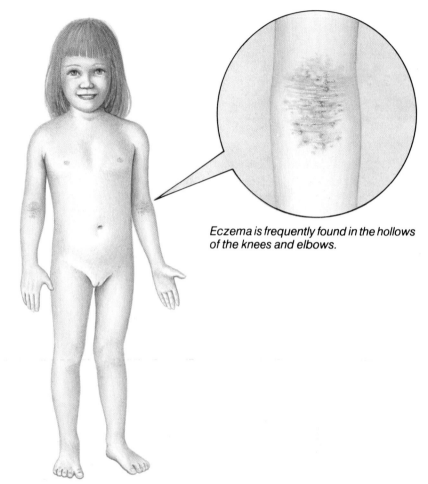

Eczema is frequently found in the hollows of the knees and elbows.

Symptoms

Eczema is a form of allergy which can affect babies as young as 2–4 months. The rash starts as small red spots on the cheeks, then spreads to the face, the hollows of the knees and elbows, the hands and sometimes over the whole body. The skin is red and irritated; sometimes it is moist, and sometimes dry and scaly. The area round the mouth is usually rash-free. The eczema sets up a constant itch, and it is sometimes hard for a child to refrain from tearing his skin with his nails and making the problem even worse.

Most children grow out of this infantile eczema when they are 1–2 years old, but sometimes it persists, especially in the hollows of the knees and elbows and in the crease of the neck.

Frequently no cause can be discovered for infantile eczema. Sometimes it is due to some food the baby is taking. If you are breast-feeding him try to avoid eating anything to which he might react, such as chocolate, eggs, fruit, nuts and shellfish. Breast-feeding should not be discontinued, because what a baby is given at the breast is less likely to produce eczema than is any other food. If the infant is also being given fruit-juice this should be discontinued, and the same applies to vitamin A and D drops, since these will sometimes make the eczema worse. If eczema breaks out when you change over from mother's milk to bottle feeding, the tinned milk is at fault. In this case ask the health centre or clinic for advice. Allergy to cow's milk can put a child in shock, with loss of colour and shivering fits. Milk allergy usually ceases after a few years. Infantile eczema can gradually develop into ordinary eczema, which is frequently found in the hollows of the knees and elbows, in the crease of the neck and round the eyes, and causes a disagreeable itching. Even in this type of eczema it can be impossible to find the causes. It frequently disappears at the age of 10 or 11.

Treatment

- Avoid foodstuffs which could cause or aggravate the condition. Remove dust-traps from the house.
- Try zinc ointment. If this does not help consult the doctor or the health centre or clinic. It is possible that you may be given a prescription for an ointment containing hydrocortisone plus medicines to reduce the irritation (antihistamines).
- In serious cases you will be referred to the paediatrician or dermatologist for further testing and intensive treatment.
- Dress the child in thin clothing, because excessive warmth will aggravate the itching. Children with eczema are sensitive to wool, and also to certain synthetic materials such as nylon. Clothes made of pure cotton are the most suitable.
- Keep the child's nails short, without cutting them down to the quick, so that he cannot tear his skin.

Asthma

This is the most dramatic of all allergic diseases, and unfortunately one of the commonest. The disease often starts when the child is a toddler, and sometimes in the first years of life.

Symptoms

The allergen is found mainly in the air the child breathes, and the antibodies occur in the bronchial tubes. The result is that the muscles in the walls of the smallest tubes contract, so that the latter become narrower. At the same time the mucous membranes swell and the mucus gets thick and sticky. The air-passages are so restricted that they make a whistling sound as the air is forced through them.

An acute attack of asthma starts as oppression in the chest. Breathing is difficult, especially breathing out. The chest expands, and you see that the child has to make an effort to keep breathing. Simultaneously you hear a hissing and whistling sound from the windpipe. The child's face turns pale and his lips can become blue, while the pulse is feeble. When the spasm in the bronchial tubes starts to subside the child expectorates large quantities of mucus.

Asthma is caused by something a child inhales – say dust, pollen, feathers, animal epithelium, or fungal spores. The commonest allergen is a mite present in every house, a microscopic organism that feeds on the dead cells shed from human skin. It is present in household dust among other things. When the beds are made, and during cleaning and dusting, large quantities of mites are thrown up into the air. Even food such as milk, fish, eggs and certain vegetables – e.g., peas – can be the cause. Surprisingly small amounts are able to bring on an attack. Sometimes all that is needed is for the child to smell the fish that is being cooked.

Many asthmatic patients are unusually sensitive to the germs that infect the respiratory passages, and also to the smell of paint, tobacco-smoke and perfumes.

Treatment

- Always consult the doctor when the symptoms indicate asthma. Apart from anything else, he can find out which allergens are causing the trouble. Once this is known you can try to keep the child from exposure to the offending substance or substances as much as possible.
- Once the diagnosis has been made it will not be necessary to alert the doctor every time a child has an attack. Nowadays effective medicines are available, both to prevent asthma and to allay an attack. The doctor will tell you when and how they have to be used.
- Some children who are allergic can be inoculated against the substance to which they react – e.g., against pollen or bee venom.
- The child will need to be shown by a physiotherapist how to breathe properly. It is also important for him to engage in a certain amount of sport so that he stays in good condition.
- Try to reduce the number of mites in the bedroom by avoiding things which create a great deal of dust, because that is where these creatures thrive. Avoid horsehair mattresses, fluffly blankets and wall-to-wall carpeting. Try to keep the house free from dust and plants as far as possible.

Remember that acute attacks of asthma must be treated by the doctor. The drugs used are sometimes given by injection. An attack can usually be terminated by effective home treatment.

Hay fever

Hay fever is frequently caused by pollen floating in the air during spring and summer. This can be the pollen of timothy-grass or other species of grass, or of trees such as the birch. The pollen of certain flowers such as the ox-eye daisy can also be to blame.

Some children are affected by the pollen of spring flowers with such a short season that the trouble is soon over, but others suffer from their allergies throughout the spring and summer. There are even some unfortunates who live with hay

fever from one year's end to the other. In this case the trouble lies in other allergens such as animal epithelium, dust, fungal spores or flowers. When the child comes in contact with the allergen his mucous membranes swell and secrete a clear fluid, while the nose itches and alternates between being blocked and runny. When the nose is runny the child sneezes and his eyes are bloodshot and sore. He feels tired and listless.

Hay fever is sometimes associated with asthma.

Treatment

- The best treatment is to avoid the allergen. When the pollen count is high the child should stay indoors as much as possible. Keep the window shut, and do not hang the clothes outside to dry.
- Many children can be inoculated against specific pollens.
- Preventive medicines – in the form of tablets, for instance – are available against hay fever. There are also nasal sprays and very effective drops for irritated eyes.

Nettle-rash
(urticaria)

Symptoms

Nettle-rash is an allergic skin reaction, mainly affecting rather older children. The rash is similar to that caused by stinging nettles – irregular white spots with a red background. The rash can cover the body and give rise to considerable irritation. When the reaction is severe the lips and eyelids can swell. Sometimes the throat likewise swells, and causes breathing difficulties. There can also be swellings without a rash. Usually both the rash and the irritation disappear after a few hours, but as soon as they disappear in one place they appear in another, and so the symptoms continue for days on end.

Sometimes an acute reaction can be so strong that the child's temperature rises to between 100·5 and 102·5°F (38–39°C). Severe reactions can occur following insect-bites.

Nettle-rash can be caused by certain foods such as strawberries, lobsters or fish. Drugs such as aspirin or penicillin can also bring on an attack.

Treatment

- The irritation can be alleviated by antihistamine preparations.
- In more serious cases cortisone is used, and this is very quick-acting. When the nettle-rash is very severe indeed adrenaline must be injected.

Insect allergies

Wasp and bee stings are especially liable to have nasty side-effects. In most instances they cause nothing more than local swelling and some irritation, but in certain children the whole hand and arm might swell up if they have been stung by a wasp on the finger, or perhaps they will come out in nettle-rash on the greater part of their bodies. In very serious cases a child can go into shock – the mucous membranes of the mouth and throat swell, the blood pressure falls and the child may become unconscious.

Treatment

- If you think your child is in shock call the doctor at once. Give artificial respiration only if necessary (see page 84).
- Make sure that you keep cortisone or antihistamine preparations in the house for immediate use after a sting if your child is allergic.
- Nowadays a course of injections spread over several years is often given to children with severe allergies in order to desensitize them.

The urinary passages

The function of the kidneys is to rid the body of unwanted metabolic products and to preserve a normal balance between salt and water. 'Healthy' urine consists of waste products and salts dissolved in water, but when the urine also contains albumen, sugar, blood, pus or bacteria something is wrong.

Infections of the urinary passages

Infections of the urinary passages are quite common in children. The trouble can affect the newborn, especially if they are boys, but in older children it is mainly girls who are at risk. The site of the infection can be the pelvis of the kidney (in which case there is a risk of kidney damage) or only the bladder or the urethra.

A ureter (A) runs from each kidney (B) to the bladder (C), where the urine is collected. The urine is expelled via the urethra (D).

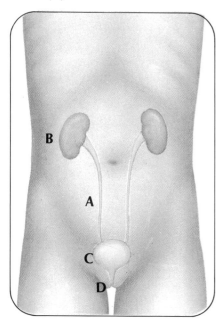

When the urinary passages are infected it is usually because bacteria from the individual's own intestines – especially the common *Escherichia coli* – have invaded them. The bacteria can also spread via blood and lymphatic vessels from other parts of the body. It is not true that a person catches a urinary-passage infection when he is cold, but a chill certainly lowers the resistance to any infection that may be present. Girls are more liable than boys to infections of the urinary passages, possibly because their urethra is shorter and wider and is in closer proximity to the rectum. Therefore it is very important to teach girls the correct way to wash and wipe themselves after going to the lavatory. They should always wash or wipe from front to back, from the opening of the urethra backwards to the anus. This reduces the risk of transferring bacteria. Wash with soap and lukewarm water, but not more often than once a day; on other occasions use lukewarm water only.

A congenital constriction in the ureters or urethra can often encourage infections, which can recur time after time.

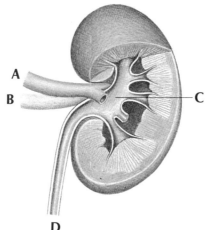

A longitudinal section through a kidney. Blood enters the kidney via the renal artery (A) in order to be filtered. The renal vein (B) then takes the filtered blood from the kidney. The pelvis of the kidney (C) collects the urine, which is conveyed via the ureter (D) to the bladder.

The course of the illness

It can be difficult to identify an infection of the urinary passages, especially in babies. Sometimes the sole symptoms are that a child is not putting on weight and is apathetic and irritable. When a child suffers from repeated bouts of fever-ishness without any other symptoms, or has a high temperature accompanied by vomiting, the underlying reason may be an infection of the pelvis of the kidney (pyelitis). Typical symptoms in somewhat older children with inflammation of the bladder (cystitis) are frequent urination accompanied by a burning sensation; they can also wet themselves suddenly. Occasionally an infection of the urinary passages occurs a few weeks after an infection of the respiratory passages, but this is exceptional.

Treatment

* If you think your child has an infection of the urinary passages, consult the doctor.
* A sample of the child's urine must be collected in a clean bottle, so that the doctor can have it examined for albumen, blood, white corpuscles and bacteria. When there are bacteria in the urine suitable antibiotics can be given, once they have been identified.
* It is preferable for the urine sample to be taken by the doctor since he will use sterile vessels and wadding, but some children find it difficult to urinate on command and in such cases it is better to collect the sample at home when they are ready. The urine should not contain bacteria from the genitals, since this would falsify the results, so make sure the child delivers the sample as cleanly as possible. Give the child a wash from the front towards the anus. Wash boys under their foreskins, although this may be difficult to do when they are little. The sample has to be stored in a cool place, preferably in the refrigerator, before delivering it to the doctor as soon as possible.

- When tests reveal that a child has an infection of the urinary passages antibiotics are usually given for 1–2 weeks.
- If a child has a high temperature he will have to stay in bed or, depending on the symptoms, remain indoors in restful surroundings. Eventually he will be able to go out of doors again as usual, but only if he does not get cold.
- Because urinary infections can recur for some months afterwards, fresh urine samples will have to be taken at intervals to monitor the situation. Occasionally a child will have to be treated with antibiotics for several months in order to prevent a second infection.
- Apart from that, X-ray plates are often made nowadays so that the kidneys and ureters can be checked for malformation – e.g., constriction – since this could lie at the root of the trouble. An operation can usually be performed for malformations of this type in order to prevent chronic damage to the kidneys.
- In some cases bacteria can be found in the urine of girls apparently unaccompanied by any ill-effects. It is becoming customary nowadays to leave this condition untreated.

Nephritis

Children, especially those from 6 to 10 years old, can contract nephritis as a complication after scarlet fever, after inflammation of the ear or throat caused by streptococci, or after impetigo. Thanks to penicillin and other antibiotics, it has become a very rare disease.

The course of the illness

The symptoms appear within a week or two of certain infections, such as those in the throat. Blood in the urine tinges it a rusty brown colour. The child feels exhausted, loses his appetite and can suffer from headaches due to high blood-pressure. In some instances there may be a degree of puffiness of the face. Occasionally the kidneys may even stop functioning.

Sometimes in addition to the inflammation of the kidneys there is bleeding beneath the skin – which gives black and blue patches known as Henoch-Schönlein's purpura – and in the intestines.

Treatment

- Always consult the doctor over a suspected case of nephritis. The child will probably be admitted to hospital, since it is important that what he eats and drinks is adjusted to the secretory power of his kidneys.
- Treatment further consists of a course of penicillin for 1 to 2 weeks. It can go on for months before the kidneys are healed.
- Prolonged monitoring will be necessary to check the progress of the cure. At least 90 per cent of all children who suffer from nephritis make a complete recovery.

Nephrosis

Nephrosis is another of those diseases of the kidney which are fortunately rare. The cause is unknown. The symptoms are fatigue and considerable puffiness, especially about the face; this is due to the escape of large quantities of albumen from the kidneys. A patient with nephrosis must always enter hospital for treatment. At one time this disease often ended in death; nowadays there is a very good chance of recovery.

Fits

Epilepsy

Epilepsy manifests itself in convulsions or fits of unconsciousness – pointing to the fact that something has interfered with the normal activity of the brain. In babies the most common causes are injuries during the foetal stage or at birth, but when the attacks first occur during the toddler stage the reasons are still far from clear. Some attacks are initiated by a head injury or meningitis. A brain tumour produces fits in children only when other symptoms such as severe headache and paralysis are present.

There are several forms of epilepsy, the commonest being *grand mal* (big fit), *petit mal* (small fit), and psychomotor epilepsy.

The course of the illness

Grand mal. The child loses consciousness, usually without warning, and falls to the ground. At the beginning of an attack the child's eyes will be fixed and staring, with pupils dilated, while his face turns purple. His teeth are tightly clenched, and foam appears on his lips. Then the whole body becomes taut and there are convulsive movements of the arms and legs in particular.

After the attack – which lasts for a few minutes – the child feels tired and wants to sleep.

Petit mal. The child looks vacant for a few seconds and then carries on as if nothing had happened. Sometimes you catch him gazing at nothing with an absent expression on his face, or you see his eyes fluttering during an attack. *Petit mal* can be hard to recognize, and sometimes is taken for inattentiveness.

Psychomotor epilepsy. The term psychomotor epilepsy is employed to describe the automatic repetition of certain movements such as picking at his clothes, vigorous chewing or some quite complicated action, in a state of reduced consciousness. The attacks last no more than a few minutes.

Treatment

A child who suffers from epileptic attacks must be examined by the doctor. Nowadays there are good drugs for lessening the severity of the fits, or even bringing about complete relief. However, these must be taken for many years.

There are several special causes of fits – e.g., low blood sugar, certain metabolic diseases and some infections. The investigation of these causes has to take place in hospital.

Infantile convulsions

Some children between the ages of 6 months and 3–5 years can suffer from convulsions whenever their temperature increases. This is due to the fact that their brains are sensitive to any rise in temperature, especially when it happens quickly. Sometimes the fits will occur as soon as the temperature reaches 100·5°F (38°C).

The course of the illness

The child becomes stiff and loses consciousness, his eyes roll up, his jaws are firmly clenched and his body jerks convulsively. The fit is usually over in a few minutes. Try to time it if possible. When the child regains consciousness he is tired, but otherwise the same as usual.

The fits tend to occur in the evening, when the temperature is naturally at its highest. Sometimes they signal the beginning of some feverish illness.

Treatment

- Try to reduce the temperature by washing the child with tepid water. When he comes round you can give him something such as junior aspirin to bring the temperature down.
- Call the doctor if it is the first time your child has had convulsions. He will be able to determine whether the attack was really one of infantile convulsions. What is more, he will be able to advise you on how to avoid a repetition of the fit.
- If an attack lasts longer than 10 to 15 minutes, if several fits follow one another in close succession, or if a fit occurs after the start of a fever, call the doctor.

Endocrine diseases

The ductless glands such as the thyroid, the adrenals and parts of the pancreas are also known as endocrine glands. Diseases of the endocrines may either be congenital or develop later. What is common to these diseases is that one of the glands produces too much or too little of a certain hormone. The commonest of these complaints in children are diabetes and thyroid disorders.

Here and there throughout the country newborn babies will be given a routine blood-test to check the functioning of the thyroid gland.

Hyperthyroidism
(overactivity of the thyroid gland)

This is a rare disease in children, and hardly ever occurs before puberty. It is found more often in girls than in boys.

The course of the illness

A goitre – i.e., an enlargement of the thyroid gland – develops, and shows itself as a swelling in the neck. Other symptoms are perspiration, tremor in the hands, palpitations of the heart, nervousness and drowsiness.

Treatment

Hyperthyroidism is treated with preparations which reduce the activity of the thyroid gland. In adults especially, fairly large sections of the enlarged gland are sometimes removed by surgery.

Hypothyroidism
(underactivity of the thyroid gland)

The course of the disease

Children who are born with a malfunctioning thyroid gland show serious symptoms in the first few months. They are sluggish and have no appetite, their skin is rough, cold and sometimes tinged with blue, and they have a hoarse voice; their abdomen is full and broad. These children are retarded physically and mentally.

The disease can also occur later, especially during puberty and more often in girls than in boys. The main symptoms are lassitude, a constant head cold and constipation.

Treatment

The child should be given thyroid hormones as soon as possible. If the treatment is started in good time most of the symptoms disappear and the child will develop fairly satisfactorily. Nowadays a blood sample is taken to determine how the thyroid gland is functioning in newborn infants. In this way defective functioning can be discovered before the symptoms appear, and the chances of a full recovery are improved.

Diabetes

Blood sugar is regulated by several hormones, the most important of which is insulin, which is manufactured by the pancreas. In diabetes not enough insulin is being produced. The level of sugar in the blood becomes too high and sugar is excreted in the urine.

Childhood diabetes can begin at any age, but generally speaking occurs in children between the ages of 3 and 5 or 8 and 10 years. The disease is inherited. The first symptoms of diabetes are poor appetite, lassitude and weight-loss. In addition, the child becomes increasingly thirsty and he has to keep passing water. He may start to wet his bed.

Treatment

A patient with diabetes will have to be admitted to hospital. There it will be possible to discover which kind of insulin and what amounts will suit him best. The child and his parents have to learn what diet has to be adopted, how injections are given, how the urine is tested, and so on.

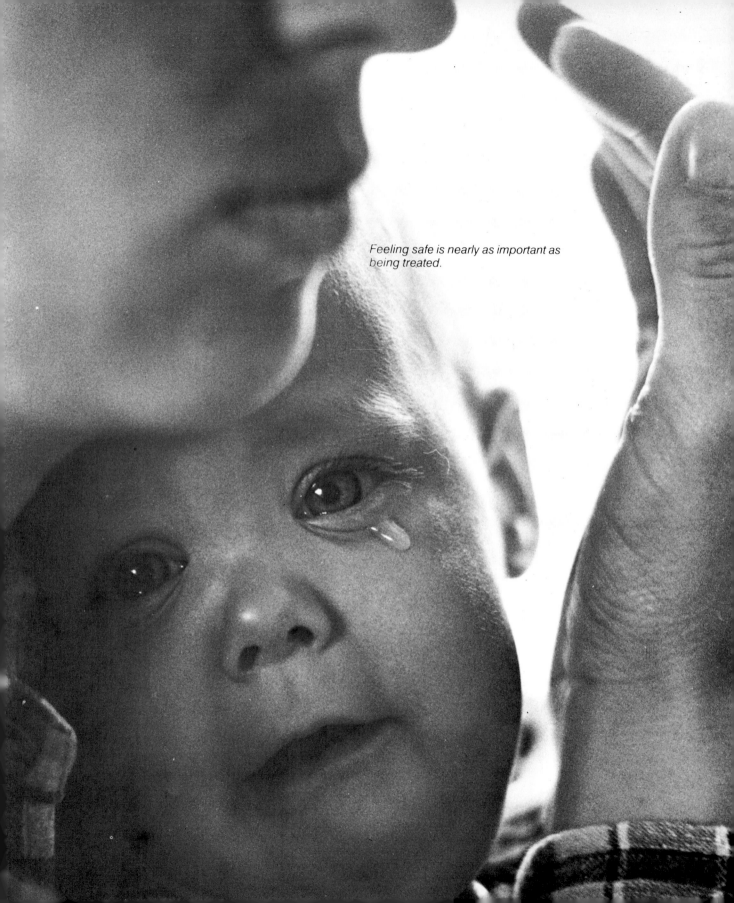

Feeling safe is nearly as important as being treated.

Injuries

Every year thousands of children are injured, sometimes fatally, in or near their homes. Pre-school children are involved in almost a third of all home accidents. Older children are more at risk on the road or outdoors.

When a child is badly injured he must receive treatment as quickly as possible. Bad wounds can endanger life or cause permanent damage. When the proper help is given quickly the consequences need not be so serious. The adjoining panel gives advice on what to do as soon as your child is injured.

Even in slight injuries it is important to give a child the right treatment in order to forestall possible complications.

First Aid

- Check whether or not the child is breathing. Do not give artificial respiration unless the breathing has stopped (see page 84).

- Make sure that the air passages are kept free. If the child is unconscious turn him so that he is lying on his side, face slightly down (see page 83).

- Stop the bleeding (see page 86).

- Prevent shock (see page 86). Badly injured children must lie down, and must be protected against heat-loss.

- Never move a badly injured child unless it is vital to do so.

- When you change the child's position, be careful not to make his injuries worse.

- Do not use your own car if your child is seriously injured. Call an ambulance as quickly as possible.

- If you have to fetch help, return to your child as quickly as possible. His condition can soon change.

Mental and emotional reactions

A sudden serious injury puts a great deal of mental and emotional stress on both your child and yourself. The child can get into a state where he screams, weeps, flies into a rage or becomes apathetic, so that it is difficult to make contact with him. An adult can panic in such a situation, and feel unable to cope. Do remember, however, that a badly injured youngster is in great need of a sense of security; you must not allow your own feelings to affect him and make matters worse. Try to remain calm, and never leave him alone unless you have to do so.

The risk of tetanus

One serious complication in the case of wounds is tetanus. Tetanus bacteria produce a poison that affects the nervous system and causes muscular spasm. After a while the respiratory muscles are affected, and the patient can die of suffocation. Since routine inoculations have been given against tetanus, the disease now rarely attacks children.

In principle, all open wounds can cause tetanus, because the tetanus bacteria are present in dirt, soil and faeces. Children who have had tetanus injections are already sufficiently protected when the injury is not too serious. Remember, however, that the protection gradually wears off, and children need to be re-inoculated when they are about 5 years of age. When a child is wounded, and the risk of tetanus seems to be high, a new injection will often be given; this quickly provides adequate protection.

When a child who has not been inoculated is injured and there is a high risk of tetanus, so-called human immune globulin can be given. An injection like this affords immediate protection apart from any vaccination, but since this protection is only short-lived the vaccination will be required to complete it.

Consult the doctor about the risk of tetanus:
- if there is a deep wound smeared with earth;
- if the wound is a stab-wound, as when a child treads on a nail;
- if a child is bitten by a dog, cat, rat, horse or another child;
- if there are burns on the feet or bottom.

Wounds

Cleaning wounds

Wash your hands carefully before dealing with a wound, and do not touch it. Use lint, not cotton wool, to clean the wound, and employ a mild soap. Apart from soap and water, you can also clean wounds with a physiological salt solution or with one of the disinfectant solutions specially prepared for cleaning wounds. Do not use this for eyes or ears, and remember that preparations for cleaning wounds should be used fresh after dilution. Do not use ointment on a wound, since this retards the healing process.

Inflamed wounds

Wounds caused by bites and wounds made dirty with soil or street dirt can easily become inflamed due to the bacteria which lodge themselves in the tissues. The edges of the wound become red and swollen, and the wound itself gets hot and throbs painfully. Often there is pus present, but do *not* squeeze it out. An inflamed wound has to be cleaned and given a clean dressing every day. If you are not sure how to treat it, ask the doctor for advice.

Infection from a wound can spread to the lymphatic vessels and glands, and cause inflammation of the lymphatic system. This is one of the body's defence mechanisms, and not blood poisoning as is often thought. A red line running from the wound to the lymph nodes (in the groin and armpits, for instance) is a sign of inflammation of the lymphatic glands. Sometimes there is an accompanying rise in temperature. In that event consult the doctor.

Serious wounds

- Extensive skin wounds
- Deep wounds – e.g., those caused by bites
- Large gaping wounds
- Very dirty wounds
- Wounds which are actively bleeding, must be treated by the doctor. The underlying tissues and organs can be affected.

Treatment

- Staunch any bleeding (see page 86).
- Do not touch the wound itself with your fingers.
- Do not try to remove firmly embedded splinters (see page 76).
- Do not wash the wound yourself.
- Wounds which have to be stitched should be treated within 6 hours.
- Treat with a first-aid dressing (see page 108) or with a piece of lint covered by adhesive plaster. If there is nothing else available, use a clean handkerchief.
- When a child is badly injured try to prevent possible shock (see page 86).
- Get in touch with the doctor or the hospital.

If the wound is very dirty, hold it under running water while carefully cleaning the surrounding skin with a nail-brush.

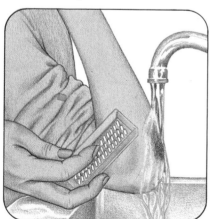

Wash the skin round the wound with mild soap and water.

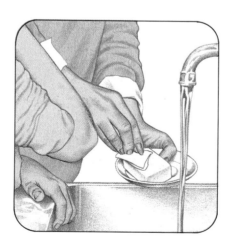

Finally clean the skin surrounding the wound, washing away from the wound.

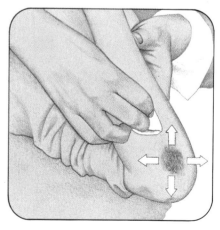

Bandaging

Various dressings

Ordinary first-aid plaster is a good dressing for small wounds. Preferably it should be water-repellent and perforated, so as not to fit the wound too tightly. It can be bought in rolls or ready-cut in various sizes. Special plasters are also available for fingers and toes.

For larger wounds it is sometimes better to use bandage. This may be purchased in different widths and qualities. (For bandaging methods see pages 67, 68.)

For wounds on the head, knees, elbows, hands and feet, lint held in place with a piece of Netelast is very effective. A dressing of this kind is easy to apply, and sits firmly in place. The Netelast material is made of thin rubber and cotton and is very elastic. It comes in various sizes.

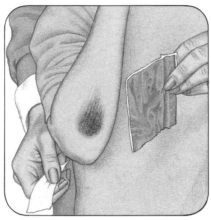

Gauze sticking-plaster

Remove the protective foil from one side of the plaster and stick the plaster to sound skin along one edge of the wound.

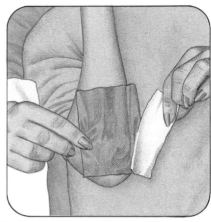

Press the other side of the plaster on to the skin along the opposite edge of the wound, while removing the second strip of foil. Never touch the medicated gauze that has to cover the wound.

Netelast

Cover the wound with a piece of lint, possibly with a wad of cotton wool on top. Stretch the Netelast with your hands inside it and push it over the wound.

Withdraw one hand while keeping the Netelast in place. Adjust the dressing if necessary. Withdraw your other hand.

The Netelast fits snugly and holds the dressing in place.

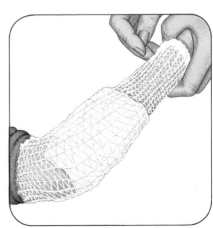

Gaping wounds

Cuts, or wounds caused by a hard knock on a place with bone just below the skin – e.g., on the forehead – often bleed very freely. The edges of such wounds often spring apart, and they heal to leave ugly scars. When the wound is deep, underlying organs such as nerves and tendons can be damaged, especially in wounds of the hands and feet.

Wounds which are more than ¾ inch (19mm) long and gape more than 1–1½ inches (25–38mm), and any gaping wounds in the face, must be treated by a doctor or nurse. In order to stop the bleeding you can lightly press a piece of lint or a clean handkerchief on the wound for a few minutes. If the wound is in an arm or a leg the limb must be raised. If the bleeding fails to stop within 10–15 minutes, consult the doctor.

The illustrations show how to dress small gaping wounds.

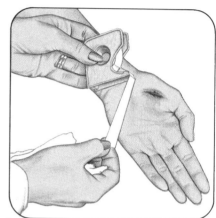

After careful cleaning you can bring the edges of the wound together with sticky plaster. This is obtainable in various widths from the chemists.

Bandaging the fingers and toes

Specially shaped Tubegauz can easily be fitted over a finger or toe with a special applicator (shown here).

Cut a piece of Tubegauz that is at least twice as long as the child's finger. Pull the whole length of gauze over the applicator.

Push the applicator and gauze over the finger and pull the gauze to the bottom of the finger.

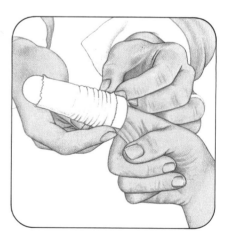

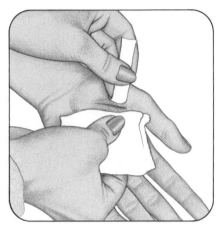

Stick the plaster securely beside one edge of the wound and push the edges of the wound together with a piece of lint. Do not touch the wound.

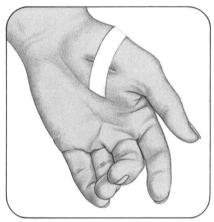

Fix the plaster to the other side of the wound. If necessary use additional strips of plaster. Place a piece of lint on top and then a wad of cotton wool.

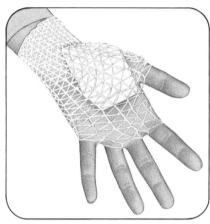

Pull a piece of Netelast over the hand and cut a hole in it for the thumb. Work the fingers carefully through the mesh.

Hold the Tubegauz firmly and pull the applicator up until it is just off the top of the finger. Then give the applicator one complete turn as shown.

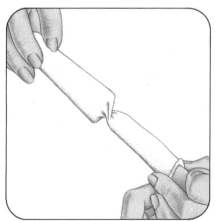

Push the applicator back down over the finger.

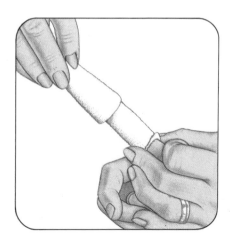

Pull the applicator off and secure the gauze with plaster.

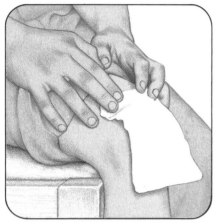 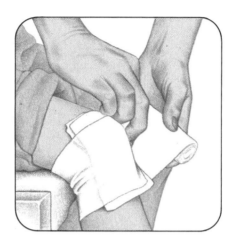 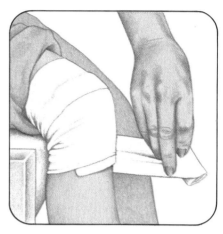

Bandaging the knee or elbow

Let your child help you to hold the dressing in place, but make sure he does not touch the part that is going to cover the wound.

First wind the bandage once or twice round the knee with the knee slightly bent.

Then make one turn above the knee and one turn below the knee so that the turns meet in the middle of the knee.

Bandaging the hand

Secure the bandage with a couple of turns round the wrist. Then wind the bandage diagonally across the palm between the angle of opening of the thumb and from there right under the fingers to the little finger.

Continue to wind the bandage round the knuckles and bottoms of the fingers several times.

Take the bandage diagonally back across the palm from the little finger to the wrist. Continue until there are no gaps between the lint and the bandage fits snugly.

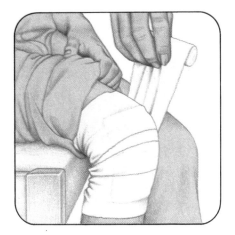

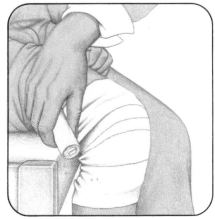

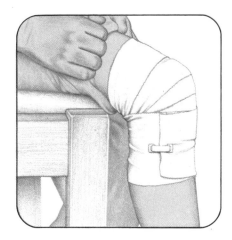

Then wind the bandage alternately above and below the knee, with the crossover in the hollow of the knee, until the first layer of bandage is completely covered.

Always leave one-third of the underlying turn exposed. The picture shows how to hold the roll.

Finish with a couple of turns around the leg. Secure the bandage with a safety-pin or with plaster. Netelast may then be pulled over the top (see page 65).

Finally wind the bandage a couple of times round the wrist and fasten with a safety-pin or plaster. Netelast may then be pulled over the top (see page 65).

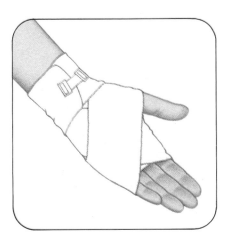

The right way to bandage

- Wash your hands before unwrapping the bandage.
- Make sure that the child is sitting or lying comfortably, and that the injured part is properly supported.
- If necessary the lint can be covered with a layer of absorbent cotton wool. This mops up liquid from the wound and gives some protection against knocks. However, do not put cotton wool directly on the wound.
- Hold a roll of bandage so that you unroll it on to the body (see illustrations).
- Do not make the bandaging too slack or too tight. After a short time check that the skin next to the bandaging is not turning darker or swelling.
- Do not change the bandage too frequently. If it is very bloodstained put a new bandage on top of the old. If it becomes dirty or wet change it very carefully so that the healing process is not delayed by the edges of the wound being dragged apart or the scab being rubbed off. Clean the wound before putting on a fresh bandage.
- Be careful what you do with old soiled bandages. Place them in a bag and tie it tightly before disposing of it.

Minor injuries

Nose-bleed

When a child receives a blow on the nose, or pokes something up it, the small blood vessels in the nasal septum are damaged, and there is a haemorrhage. Sometimes the child's nose will bleed as a complication in an infection, but it can also start to bleed without provocation. Bleeding of this kind is not dangerous, and is quite easy to stop. If your child suffers from *repeated* nose-bleeds for no obvious reason you must consult the ear, nose and throat specialist.

Treatment

- Sit the child upright. Pinch the nostrils firmly together for 10–15 minutes. Allow the child to spit out the blood that runs into his throat, otherwise he could be sick.
- If the bleeding does not stop after 15 minutes of firm pressure get in touch with the doctor.
- When the bleeding has stopped the child must not pick his nose or blow his nose hard for a while.

Pinch the nostrils firmly together.

A pinched nail

A pinched nail or a blow on the nail can be painful. The pain is due to the blood collecting under the nail.

If you act promptly and press on the nail for a few minutes the bleeding can be reduced. While doing this keep the hand or foot raised.

If the pain does not get better, the pressure under the nail will have to be relieved. Take the child to the casualty department or the doctor.

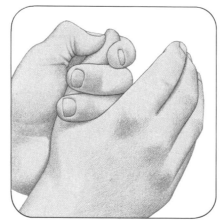

Squeeze the nail for a couple of minutes to reduce the bleeding.

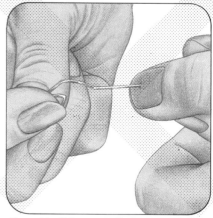

Do not try this yourself – leave such forms of relief to the doctor.

Bruises

Small children are very liable to hit their heads on the corners of tables, doorposts and other hard objects, and have frequent falls when they start to walk. The bleeding caused by these accidents stays in the tissues below the skin and causes a swollen blue patch – a bruise.

The bleeding – and therefore the swelling and pain – can be reduced by pressing the bruise with the hand, or better still with something cold such as an ice-cube wrapped in a handkerchief. This has to be done for 5–10 minutes to do any good.

Bites and stings

Bites

How you treat a wound caused by the bite of a cat, dog, or other mammal depends on the depth of the wound and on whether or not the child has been inoculated against tetanus (see page 63). Usually the wound is superficial, and all that need be done is to clean and bandage it. If the wound is deep or in the face, or if you are not sure that the child has been effectively inoculated against tetanus, consult the doctor.

Children can also bite each other, and these wounds can be treated in the same way as animal bites.

Adder-bites

Adder-bites always cause a local reaction. Within a few hours the part of the body that has been bitten swells and turns a reddish-blue. The effect of these bites on children is often very serious. They turn pale, feel sick and have a weak and rapid pulse. They may also become unconscious.

Treatment

- Remain calm. An adder-bite does not threaten life directly.
- See to it that the child is kept quiet and does not get cold. Above all, make sure he rests the part of the body that was bitten as much as he can.
- Wrap a bandage at least 2 inches (50 mm) wide above the bite (e.g., on a leg) but make sure it is not too tight.
- Do not finger the bite. It is a great mistake to squeeze or suck it.
- Go to the hospital as quickly as possible. If a child has not been inoculated there is a risk of tetanus. If you are out for the day in summer and a long way away from the nearest hospital, it can be helpful to give cortisone tablets before the journey there. This drug has to be prescribed by a doctor.

Bee and wasp stings

- With bee and wasp stings, the skin round the place which was stung becomes red and swollen. The pain can be alleviated by dabbing on a cooling lotion such as calamine. If the child is in a good deal of pain, give one of the usual pain-killers.
- In bee-stings the barb is often left behind. Remove it with tweezers.
- Always go to a doctor or the hospital if the child has proved hypersensitive to stings in the past, or the sting is in the mouth or throat.
- Consult the doctor if the child is under the age of three and has been stung several times on the same occasion.

Removing the sting or barb

Barbs which have lodged themselves in the skin must be removed as quickly as possible. Using a pair of blunt tweezers, take a firm grip on the sting and turn it in an anticlockwise direction until it is extracted. Do *not* tug it straight out, as the tip could be left behind to cause persistent irritation. Another method is to dab the wound liberally with cooking oil. When this is done the barb will sometimes work itself loose and slip out.

Gnats and ants

Even the more harmless bites of midges, mosquitoes and ants are sometimes troublesome to children. A cooling ointment is useful for soothing the irritation or the burning sensation.

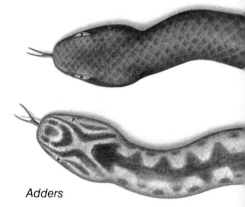

Adders

Burns

The wounds known as burns can be caused both by hot things such as boiling water, steam, or hot metal, and by chemicals such as concentrated acids or alkalis. The degree of the burn depends on the duration of the burning and the amount of heat involved. A burn, however slight, is very painful, while a severe one often involves long and painful treatment.

Treatment

- **For burns due to hot water or hot objects:**
  Hold the burnt part under a rapid flow of water for *at least* 10 minutes.
- **For burns due to hot oil or other slow-flowing substances:**
  Place the child in a bath of cold water as quickly as possible, and leave him there for at least ten minutes. Do not remove his clothes, as this may cause further damage to the burnt skin.

When a burn covers more than 9 per cent of the body surface there is a danger of shock. The calculation is based on the palm of the hand, which is about 1 per cent of the body surface.

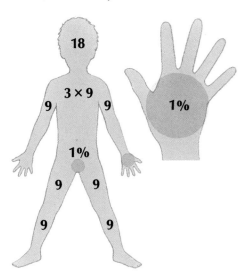

- **For burns caused by an open fire:**
  If the clothes are alight extinguish the flames with a blanket, mat or something similar. Lay the child down and take care that the flames are kept off his face. Work downward from head to toe.

  If you are trying to extinguish the fire with water, use plenty of it. If the clothes are sticking to the child's body, do not try to pull them off. Wrap the child in a clean sheet or something similar and get him to hospital in an ambulance as quickly as possible.

The seriousness of the burn

This is determined by:
- The degree of the burn;
- The surface area of the burn;
- The part of the body affected.

The surface area of the burn

In burns the surface area is expressed as a percentage of the total body surface. In a child, the palm of the hand represents 1 per cent of the body surface.

Burns occupying no more than 2 per cent of the body surface are called minor burns, and those occupying more than 2 per cent are called major burns.

The degree of the burn

First degree (superficial burns):
Very red. The burnt area may be swollen. Burning pain.

Second degree (superficial burns):
Very red, blisters, swelling of the burnt area, burning pain.

Third degree (deep burns):
Very red, blisters, swelling. The skin can be greyish-white or black, charred or leathery. Burning pain.

If a child has burnt himself with a hot liquid or some hot object, hold the burnt part under quickly flowing cold water for at least 10 minutes.

Danger of shock

- In second-degree burns covering more than 9 per cent of the body surface.
- In third-degree burns, even when they are on only a small area of skin.

Always take the child to hospital

- For burns on the face, on joints, on the buttocks or on the hands and feet.
- For third-degree burns or burns covering more than 2 per cent of the body surface.
- For small burns, if the child is feverish, the pain increases or other indications of infection exist.

  During the ride to the hospital, protect the wound with a clean bandage. In major burns you can use a sheet or tablecloth or something similar. Remember the danger of shock, and do your best to prevent it.

Treatment

Treat small burns or scalds which do not cover more than 2 per cent of the body surface as follows:

- Wash your own hands.
- Wash the skin around the burn very carefully with soap and water if it appears dirty.
- Be careful not to break the blisters on the skin. Cover them with a clean dressing.
- Hold the dressing in place with a bandage or sticking plaster. The bandage must be firm but not too tight. It can be left in place for several days unless it appears soiled.
- Never use flour, butter, ointments or any other old-fashioned domestic remedies. They can do nothing but make the wound worse.

Electric shock

If a child has been injured by electricity, it can be a matter of seconds if he is to be saved. The effect of the current on the muscular system can cause a cramp that 'glues' the child to the electrically alive equipment. Spasm in the respiratory passages can make it impossible for the child to call for help. The function of the heart can be disturbed.

Treatment

- Do not go looking for the mains switch if it is not close by; this wastes too much time. Break the current by pulling the plug out or by knocking the equipment away from the child's body. If this does not succeed, try to drag the child away, using a mat, tablecloth or something similar that you have looped round his arm or body. Do not touch the child with your hands, as he may be carrying a heavy electric charge.
- Give artificial respiration if necessary.
- Stimulate the heart if it has stopped beating (see page 85).
- Go to the hospital by ambulance as quickly as possible.

Sunburn

Sunburn is a first-degree burn. Do not expose small children to fierce sunlight; make them wear sun-hats and T-shirts. Get them used to the sun gradually.

Never rub the child with oil while he is in the sun, but use a sun-tan lotion before he goes out in it.

If the skin has been exposed to the sun for a long time and is painful, use a cooling lotion such as calamine.

Blisters

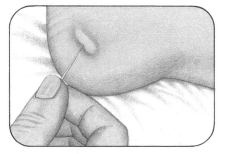

If a child has a blister, prick its outer edge with a clean needle to release the liquid.

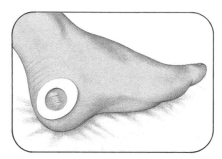

Wash the place with soap and water and protect it with a corn-ring covered with a small plaster.

Over-exposure to cold

Children quite often suffer from the effects of severe cold, but if the correct measures are taken this can usually be prevented.

When it is very cold out of doors children should wear several layers of clothing: dress them in cotton underwear and a blouse, shirt or T-shirt, with a thick sweater on top of a windproof coat and a long pair of warm trousers. Put a pair of thick tights and warm socks on them, plus a pair of waterproof leather boots. The hat or bonnet must not be too tight, and the scarf must not cover the mouth or chin, because the breath might make it damp enough to form ice that could hurt the face. The gloves must not be wet, so always take a spare pair. In fact it is a good idea for the child to wear a second, stouter pair over mitts. Do not let a child suck a dummy or bottle-teat when out of doors, and do not wash his face just before he goes out as this will remove the skin's natural protective grease. A few hours before he goes out, smear his face with an anhydrous (water-free) greasy ointment – but remember, not immediately before, because if the ointment has not been absorbed it will hinder normal transpiration and do more harm than good. The moisture trapped between the skin and the layer of cream could form ice crystals which would injure the skin.

Do not let the child go out in the cold on an empty stomach, and take a vacuum flask full of something hot to drink if you are going on a long journey. Bear in mind that a strong wind cools the body down quickly, so make sure that the child keeps on the move. It is particularly important for the facial muscles, fingers and toes to be kept moving.

Every now and then, check the colour of the child's face, especially on the forehead, cheeks, nose, chin and ears. Make sure that he does not lose the feeling in his fingers and toes.

The local effects of cold

In superficial damage due to cold, only the skin is affected. The child complains of a burning or itching sensation. His skin turns white and numb, and sometimes becomes swollen. More serious is when the cold penetrates to the underlying tissues. The skin can then turn white or as pale as wax with blue-black patches, and feels hard. The frostbite is deep when the skin does not regain its normal colour and feeling within 30 minutes of treatment. Bear in mind that the cold can cause injury even when the outside temperature is above freezing, if the wind is blowing hard and the weather is damp and the child cannot keep sufficiently active.

When you are out of doors and your child has been affected by the cold

- Try to find somewhere to shelter from the wind.
- Loosen tight clothing.
- Warm the affected parts of the child's body with your own body heat. For instance, you can use your hand to warm his chin or cheek, or you can put his frozen hand or foot under your armpit or on your stomach.
- Try to get the child to move the frozen parts.
- Give him something warm to drink.
- When normal feeling and colour have returned to the skin make sure that the part of the body affected does not freeze again.
- Never rub or chafe sores caused by cold. The skin is very sensitive, and the trouble can easily be made worse.

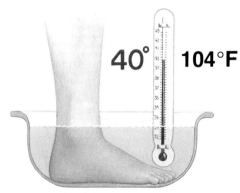

40° 104°F

With superficial damage due to cold, keep the affected part dipped in water at 40°C (no hotter).

When you are out of doors and you see that your child is suffering from the cold, you can help him by warming the affected part with your own body heat.

General lowering of body temperature

In general cooling – which can occur in someone who has been out in the cold for a long time or in cases of drowning – the temperature of the organs themselves is lowered. One of the first signs of freezing is that a child does not want to walk any further. He starts shivering and shuddering, and tries to lie down. Finally his breathing can become irregular and even stop.

Treatment for general fall in temperature

- Quickly put the child into dry clothes or wrap him in dry blankets.
- Make sure he is breathing properly; if not use artificial respiration (see page 84).
- If he is conscious, see if he is willing to move about.
- Give him something to drink in small quantities, *not too hot*.

- If the child is unconscious, turn him partly on his side (see page 83).
- Take the child to hospital as quickly as possible.
- If it is impossible to get the child to hospital within the first three hours, try to bring him indoors somewhere else, and give him first aid as described below.

What to do while waiting for the ambulance

- The warming must take place slowly at ordinary room temperature.
- Dress the child in dry clothes.
- Put him to bed and raise the foot of the bed a little in order to prevent shock.
- If the child is fully conscious, give him something lukewarm and sweet to drink, with a dash of whisky or brandy in it.
- Keep him under constant observation. There may be changes in the degree of consciousness and in respiration. If this is so, turn him slightly over on his side (see page 83).

- Make sure that the child does not get any colder while on the way to hospital.

When attempting to warm a frozen child do not use radiated heat such as is given off by an open fire, electric blankets or hot-water bottles; do not give him a hot bath or pile on bedclothes as you might do if he were just 'feeling a bit cold'. The effect of these measures is to bring about an expansion of the superficial blood-vessels in the skin. The warmer blood in the interior of the body then quickly flows to these expanded blood-vessels and cools down. When this cooled blood returns to the heart and other organs, they are subjected to further cooling. The body temperature can then fall in a few minutes, and the child's condition can deteriorate dramatically.

Foreign bodies

Foreign bodies in the nose, etc.

Children often poke things into their noses and ears, and even into their private parts. You must take special care not to push the object in further while trying to extract it.

Foreign bodies in the nose often cause foul-smelling discharge mixed with blood.
Foreign bodies in the ear can impair the hearing and cause discharge.
Foreign bodies in the vagina eventually cause yellow or yellow-green, foul-smelling discharge.
Foreign bodies in the urethra can easily slip into the bladder in girls. The child then finds urinating painful, and there is often blood in the urine.

Always consult the doctor in cases of this kind.

Broken glass in the foot

Never try yourself to remove splinters of glass embedded in the foot.

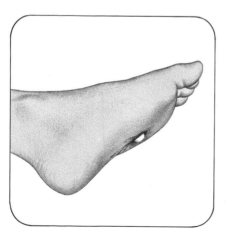

Foreign bodies which have been swallowed

In some instances foreign bodies which have been swallowed can stick in the oesophagus (the gullet). The child complains of pain in the chest, and refuses to eat or drink. Foreign bodies which have been swallowed usually enter the stomach and work their way into the bowels, eventually passing out with the motions. What the child does in his pot should be checked.

Never give laxatives.

Treatment

- Take the child to the hospital if you think anything is stuck in his gullet.
- If he has swallowed something sharp, give him asparagus or rhubarb to eat. You can also tease out a little cotton wool and mix it with cream or porridge. This will wrap itself round the sharp object and prevent it from injuring the wall of the intestines.
- If the child complains of stomach-ache or abdominal pain take him to the hospital.

Make a circle of cloth – e.g., using a handkerchief or piece of lint – or cut a ring from foam rubber.

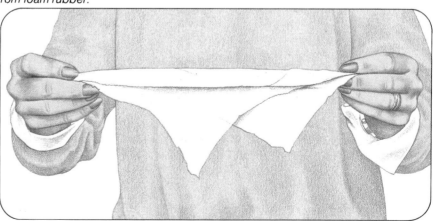

Splinter wounds

If your child steps on some sharp object that penetrates deep into his foot – for instance, a piece of broken glass or a nail – you must not try to remove it, since this may well make matters worse.

Before bandaging the wound encircle it with some sort of ring. This can be made from a handkerchief or piece of lint or from foam rubber. The ring will prevent the splinter from being driven farther into the foot. Then go to the doctor.

Injuries of this kind bring the risk of tetanus (see page 63).

When a barbed fish-hook enters the skin do not try to pull it out in one go as this could cause a very nasty wound. It is better to bring the point of the hook out through the skin in a curving motion and to snip off the barbs with a pair of pincers. The rest of the hook can then be extracted quite easily.

Eye injuries

In spite of the fact that the eye is very well protected in its socket, it can be easily injured.

Specks of dirt

Use a matchstick covered with a small pad of cotton wool to push the lid gently upwards and remove the speck very carefully with the corner of a clean handkerchief moistened with a drop or two of water. You can also try rinsing with water. Pour the water from a jug so that it flows gently over the eye.

If the eye is red and sore and watery the next day, consult the doctor.

Foreign bodies

Never try to remove anything that is stuck in the eye. Cover both eyes with a clean bandage and go to the doctor or to the casualty department. Never put cotton wool over the eyes.

If the eye has been injured with something sharp like a knife or a fragment of glass, extreme care must be taken as the child is being driven to hospital. It is particularly important to make sure that he does not bend over.

Liquids

When a child has had some dangerous liquid splashed in his eye it is best to wash the eye under a gentle stream of water for 15 to 20 minutes. Unless it becomes red, sore or watery, there is no need to go to the doctor.

Acid, alkali, mortar, quicklime

These are very dangerous. Wash out immediately and very thoroughly with whatever you have at hand – e.g., water, milk or beer. Then go to the doctor.

A blow on the eye

A blow on the eye can cause bleeding. Go to the hospital or doctor if the child has any pain or sees indistinctly.

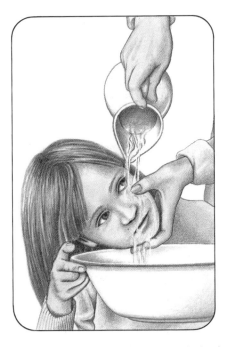

If a dangerous liquid has been splashed into the eye, wash it out with water or whatever is handy. Pull the eyelids apart so the whole eye can be rinsed. Specks of dirt can also be washed out of the eye in this way.

Place the ring round the wound and the splinter of glass. Then bandage.

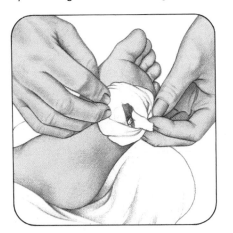

Falls

Children very easily fall and hurt themselves. Usually it is nothing serious, but sometimes they can bang their heads, injure their backs or break a leg. If you think that your child has been badly injured you must handle him very carefully so that the trouble does not become worse.

Do not move him unless it is absolutely essential. Make sure that the respiratory passages are free, and that the child is breathing properly. Give artificial respiration if necessary (see page 84).

Remember that an unconscious child must not lie on his back. Turn him partly on his side.

Head injuries

Concussion

Even after a minor blow on the head, a child can have symptoms of concussion. After a period of unconsciousness, he has a headache, he looks pale and feels giddy and sick. He may vomit and be unable to recall what has happened to him. Bear in mind that the symptoms can vary from case to case. The longer the period of unconsciousness, the graver is the brain damage. If you suspect that your child has concussion, make him lie down and rest, preferably turned slightly on his side and with *no* pillow under his head. Telephone the doctor for advice.

Brain haemorrhage

Following a blow on the head, a child can suffer from a very serious complication in the form of brain haemorrhage. The symptoms appear after several hours and sometimes after several days; the commonest symptoms are a severe headache and unconsciousness. The pulse is slow and strong. Convulsions can occur at the same time and breathing can be affected. There may be bleeding from the nose or ear, but you must not attempt to stop bleeding of this kind. You must tell the doctor about the bleeding if it has stopped before the child is seen in hospital.

Treatment

- Lay the child partly on his side (see page 83). He must lie flat. If the head hangs down, the bleeding can be made worse.
- If the child is wounded, bandage him.
- Prevent cooling by putting a blanket under and over the child.
- Make sure that the child can rest undisturbed. It is best not to leave him by himself because he may start vomiting, or his condition might deteriorate.
- Get him to hospital by ambulance as quickly as possible.

Back injuries

- If you suspect that a child has a broken spine you must take the greatest possible care. Symptoms pointing to spinal injury are a pricking sensation in the back or legs, stiffening of the legs, numbness or paralysis.

Treatment

- Leave the child lying where he is, in the same position, until the ambulance arrives. Never sit him up, and never bend his back.
- If the child is unconscious lay him very carefully on his side so that the air-passages remain open. This is best done by several people working together, so that the spine is displaced as little as possible. Another method of keeping the air passages free is to raise the lower jaw.
- Respiration can also be impeded if one of the cervical vertebrae (bones in the neck) is broken. Give artificial respiration.
- Get the child to hospital by ambulance as quickly as possible.

Broken bones

Children quite often break their bones. A break may be a *simple fracture* in which the skin is not involved, or a *compound fracture* in which the broken ends pierce the skin.

The symptoms of a broken bone are that the leg rapidly thickens at the place where the break occurred, and that movement and any attempt to support the weight of the body on the leg causes great pain. Sometimes it is obvious that the leg has been fractured, but the exact place of a fracture can be difficult to locate because the symptoms are not clear-cut. Often there is a split rather than a clear break. If you think that your child has broken a leg you must proceed with the utmost caution. Do not shift his position unnecessarily. If the *upper arm* or the *leg* has been broken, the child must be taken to hospital by ambulance. Never use a splint if the ambulance has access to the place of the accident. If you are obliged to move the child yourself, do not do so without applying a temporary splint first (see page 80).

If it is the *lower arm* or the *wrist* that has been broken, the child can be taken to hospital by car. The limb must be properly splinted in order to spare the child needless pain, and to prevent the injury from becoming worse.

In a *compound fracture* bandaging is always necessary in order to prevent infection. First apply a clean dressing to the wound. Then make a ring from a bandage, cotton wool or the like and place it around the injury – this will help the pain. The ring must be big enough to avoid touching the wound. Finally, bandage the limb or put it in a sling.

Splints

Use a piece of cardboard as a support, folding it round the arm.

Wind a bandage or shawl round the newspaper and the arm. Support the arm with a three-cornered sling or with a shawl that has been folded into a triangle. The sling is placed under the broken arm with the apex at the elbow and one of the other vertices over the shoulder of the sound arm.

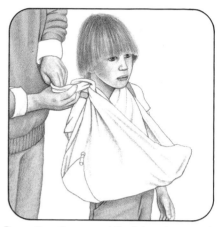

Draw the sling round the injured arm and fasten the other vertex securely at the shoulder. Fold the apex round the elbow and fasten it with a safety-pin. The hand must be higher than the elbow. Prop up the hand with a roll of bandage or something similar.

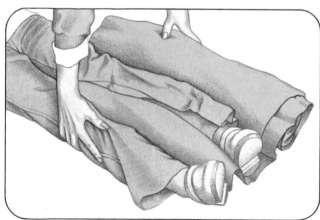

To relieve the pain and to prevent the leg slipping out of its bandage, you can support it with a small blanket, or something similar, which you can roll up and place on either side of the leg. Place the sound leg next to the broken one as a support.

If it is essential to move the child yourself, make a temporary splint. Use anything suitable, such as skis, pieces of wood or stiff cardboard. Wrap the splint in a jersey or something similar so as not to hurt the skin.

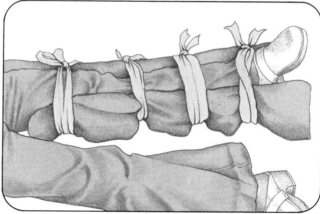

Bind the splint and leg to one another with bandages, shawls, belts etc. The splint must be long enough to support the limb above and below the break. Do not remove the shoes or boots, because these give a certain amount of support.

Sprains

When something tears in the ligaments of the wrist (for example) small haemorrhages occur, so that the skin becomes swollen and sometimes discoloured. This is called a sprain. The child finds the joint painful and difficult to move. It is especially easy to sprain an ankle.

Treatment

- Let the child sit with his foot raised for 10–15 minutes.
- Bind the ankle with a crêpe bandage – see below.
- The foot will not swell so much if you place a plastic bag containing ice-cubes on it, or get the child to sit with his foot in cold water for half an hour before bandaging.
- Keep the child off his sprained foot for a day or two.

- If the foot is swollen and painful after a couple of days, consult the doctor.
- If the child suffers severe pain, and if the foot becomes very swollen and dis-coloured, take him to hospital.

Dislocations

A dislocation is more serious than a sprain, but fortunately is not so common in children. In such injuries the bones which make up the joints lose contact with one another. The contour of the joint may change and there will be severe swelling. The child is unable to move his arm or to stand on his leg and is in great pain.

If you tug a child's arm or lift it awkwardly you can easily put it out of joint. The bone fitting loosely in the elbow joint (known as the radius) can slip out of place so that the arm hangs slack and the child cannot move his elbow. Never attempt to set a joint – in trying to put it back in place you could do an enormous amount of harm. Support the arm with, say, a crêpe bandage, and go to the doctor.

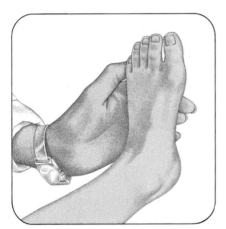

Bandaging a sprain

Support the sole of the foot with your hand and hold the foot upright while putting a crêpe bandage on it.

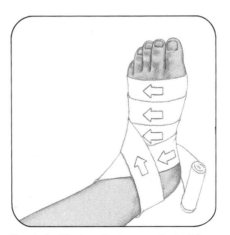

Begin just below the toes and wind the bandage round the foot. With each new turn cover about ²/₃ of the previous turn. Take care that no gaps are left between the turns, which are criss-crossed in front

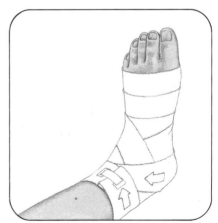

of the ankle and then run straight down underneath the foot. The heel is covered next, and finally a small section of the lower leg; the bandage is then fastened with a safety pin.

Unconsciousness

A child may lose consciousness in accidents and illnesses. The brain is affected, and is not reacting normally. Various levels of unconsciousness are distinguished.

Stupor. The child answers when something is said to him, but speaks indistinctly and incoherently.

Superficial unconsciousness. The child does not speak when spoken to, and he cannot be roused. The muscles are tensed, you can see unconscious movements and hear unconscious sounds. The child's eyes may be open, and he reacts to pain and touch. The coughing and swallowing reflexes are weak. Superficial unconsciousness can last a short time, as in fainting fits.

Deep unconsciousness. This is an extremely serious condition caused by severe external and internal injuries or by a severe illness. The muscles are tensed and the child no longer reacts to pain or touch. The coughing and swallowing reflexes are very weak, and sometimes absent. If a child in this state lies on his back there is a great danger that he may stop breathing because his tongue could fall back into the throat and block the air-passages. If vomit is produced or if blood flows into the trachea the child will not be able to cough it up.

Treatment

- Loosen tight clothing.
- Place a blanket or piece of clothing under the child.
- Turn the child to lie partly on his side.
- If for some reason it is not possible to turn a child on his side, bend his head backward to keep the air-passages open. Clean out the mouth if necessary.
- Check that the child is breathing normally.
- Never give an unconscious child anything to drink.
- Go by ambulance to the hospital.

Fainting fits

Fainting fits are short periods of unconsciousness due to a disturbance in the blood circulation that deprives the brain of oxygen. The child turns pale, can complain of sickness, dizziness and ringing in the ears, and he may see everything fade into blackness.

Fainting can be prevented if the child sits down quickly and bends his head and chest forward to help the blood flow back to the brain. A child who has fainted will recover more quickly if you lift up his legs. Make sure, however, that his head is turned to one side so that if he vomits he will not choke. Afterwards let him rest for a while to avoid another fainting fit. If consciousness has not returned within a couple of minutes, turn him over on his side.

If a child has inexplicable, prolonged fainting fits, or is subject to repeated attacks, get him to the hospital by ambulance.

A child who has fainted will recover more quickly if his legs are raised. Turn his head to one side at the same time.

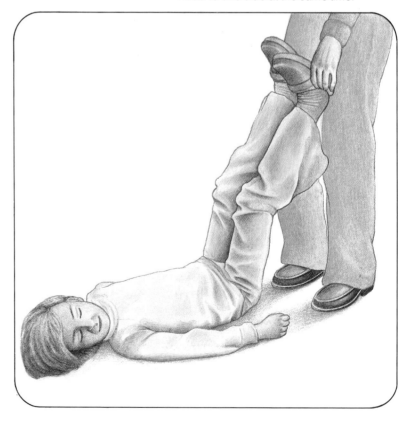

Turning the patient over

Kneel down beside the unconscious child. Turn his face towards you. Push the arm on your side under his body, with the palm of his hand facing upward.

When a child is unconscious the tongue can drop backward and block the air-passages.

Bend the leg on your side and push its foot under his other leg. Place the child's other arm so that his hand rests on the shoulder nearest you. Turn the child towards you.

To open the air-passages, hold the back of the child's neck firmly with one hand and the forehead with the other and bend the head back as far as possible.

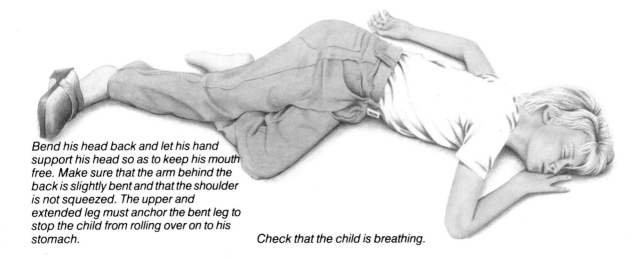

Bend his head back and let his hand support his head so as to keep his mouth free. Make sure that the arm behind the back is slightly bent and that the shoulder is not squeezed. The upper and extended leg must anchor the bent leg to stop the child from rolling over on to his stomach.

Check that the child is breathing.

When a child stops breathing

Mouth-to-mouth resuscitation

When a child is unable to breathe, saving his life becomes a matter of seconds. Brain damage can occur after only 2–3 minutes of oxygen shortage. Therefore the first thing to check is whether or not the child is breathing.

Lay your cheek close to his mouth. Can you feel his breath on your cheek? Can you see the breathing action of his chest? If not, start artificial respiration as quickly as possible. If a child is drowning, you must start while he is still in the water. Any water in the lungs will be expelled with the air after you have blown into the mouth several times. After that, turn the child's head on one side and clean out his mouth. With small children the rate at which air is blown into the mouth is 20–30 times per minute; with schoolchildren it is 18–20 times per minute. Continue until the child is breathing again. With children under three years old, blow simultaneously through the nose and mouth. Draw a normal breath and carefully blow the air in. The point about being careful is that in small children the air can find its way into the stomach, and then the abdomen swells. This can be both seen and felt. If this happens turn the child's head to one side and press the air back by cautiously pressing with your hand on his abdomen just below the ribs in the midline (the epigastrium or 'pit of the stomach').

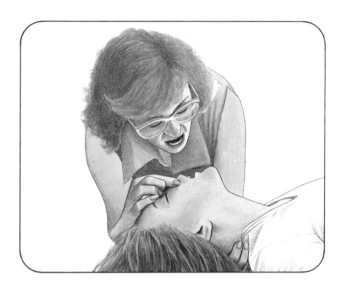

Lay the child on her back. Loosen the clothes round her neck. Hold her neck firmly with one hand and her forehead with the other. Bend her head back as far as possible to keep the air-passages free. Close the nose firmly with your thumb and index finger. Draw a deep breath.

Hang the child over your arm and pat him smartly between the shoulder blades a few times.

Foreign bodies in the air-passages

When a child has difficulty in breathing and you think that a foreign body is lodged in his air-passages, you must act quickly, because of the danger of suffocation. Loosen the clothing around the neck. If there is anything in the mouth remove it with your fingers. If this does not help, proceed as follows. Lay small children over your shoulder. Bigger children can hang over your arm, or over your lap if you are seated. Give the child several smart pats between the shoulder blades. While you are doing this the child's head must hang forward and downward a little.

Feel with your fingers inside the mouth to see if you can snatch the foreign body out. Take care that you do not press it back farther, and that you do not scratch the throat with your nails.

If you do not succeed in getting the foreign body out, and if the child's breathing is still distressed, you must use artificial respiration. By blowing forcefully, you can make the air slip past the foreign body. Foreign bodies lodged in the trachea may be forced down into one of the bronchi; the child will then be able to breathe again. When this happens you must try to stop the foreign body being forced up again. Make the child sit up straight, and try to soothe him so that he neither cries nor coughs. Then take him to hospital as quickly as possible.

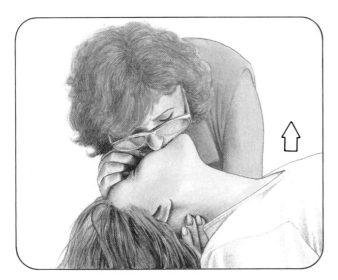

Cover the child's mouth with your own and blow air into it. Watch what happens to the child's chest. It must rise when the air is blown in.

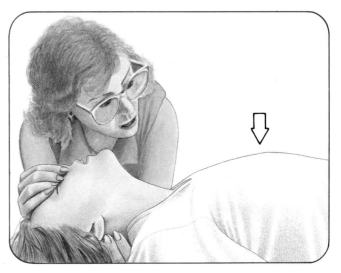

Lift your head away and breathe in at the moment the child breathes out and her chest falls.

Cardiac arrest

If a child stops breathing the heart may stop due to lack of oxygen. The pumping action of the heart can also be interrupted – by an electric shock, for example. When a child shows signs that his heart has stopped (cardiac arrest) you must try to start it working again at once. **This must be done within seconds**.

Signs of cardiac arrest

- Cessation of breathing.
- The pulse no longer beats (the beating of the pulse must be checked by feeling the artery of the neck or of the groin).
- Grey face.
- Blue lips and nails.
- Within a few minutes the pupils of the eyes dilate and do not react to light.

Treatment

Always take the child to hospital, even when he is still breathing.
- Lay the child on a hard surface. Place a cushion under his legs so that the blood can flow to the heart more quickly.
- Blow air into the mouth and lungs 3 or 4 times in order to supply oxygen.
- Check the pulse and the reaction of the pupils to light (raise an eyelid).
- If there is no pulse and the pupil does not react to light, you must strike quite hard with your clenched fist once or twice on the breast-bone at the height of the nipples. Strike from a height of about 8 inches (200 mm) with the thumb upward. The blows start the heart muscle quivering, and this can set the heart in motion.

  In babies it is sufficient to press the breast-bone with a couple of fingers. The fingers must be held straight.

- Follow up with artificial respiration until the child is breathing automatically. Then lay him partly on his side.
- The child must be taken to hospital by ambulance straight away. Continue with artificial respiration during the ride to hospital if necessary.
- Heart stimulation is not free from risk, and a faulty technique can seriously injure the ribs, liver or spleen. Further measures will have to be taken by qualified personnel.

Bleeding and shock

Stopping a haemorrhage

A distinction is made between two kinds of haemorrhage, the *internal invisible haemorrhage* – e.g., in the abdomen, muscles and inside the skull (bleeding which finds its way out through an opening in the body is also classed as internal) – and the *external haemorrhage* due to wounds.

Most haemorrhages cease spontaneously. Bleeding from an arm or leg is easier to stop when the limb is raised. At the same time a clean handkerchief or piece of gauze and lint can be carefully pressed against the wound. However, this will not be enough to staunch heavy bleeding. Then you must press the edges of the wound together with the fingers, while making sure that the injured part is higher than the rest of the body. Keep pressing the wound until you are able to make a compression bandage (see the illustrations). Make the child lie down while you are applying the bandage. Raise the bleeding part a little. If the child complains that the wound feels stiff and sore, loosen the bandage slightly but do not remove it. Prevent shock, and get the child to hospital by ambulance as quickly as possible.

A tourniquet may be applied only if an arm or leg has just been lost. It is put on as close to the injury as possible, and must not be moved before the child has been admitted to hospital. A part that has been severed from the body is best wrapped in a clean piece of cloth or something similar and taken along to the hospital. Small parts such as a finger-tip or ear-lobe can be placed in cold water in a plastic bag.

Treating shock

After a serious accident children can suffer from shock, which can be fatal. Large internal or external haemorrhages, or dehydration in burns, for example, through loss of fluid, can mean that the heart receives too little blood to keep it working. The body's organs – in particular the brain – then suffer from a lack of oxygen. The chance of shock is increased if the child also suffers from respiratory difficulties. Exertion, cooling and severe pain can also make shock more likely. Typical symptoms of shock are shivering fits, restlessness, cold hands and feet, a weak rapid pulse and quick, shallow breathing. If the child's state deteriorates he will look grey and his lips will turn blue. He will complain of thirst, and be so feeble that he can lose consciousness at any moment. In this case the child must be taken to hospital immediately because his life is in danger. When an accident has happened you must try to prevent shock.

Compression bandage

Raise your arm and press the edges of the wound together with your fingers.

The position in which a child must lie when he is unconscious.

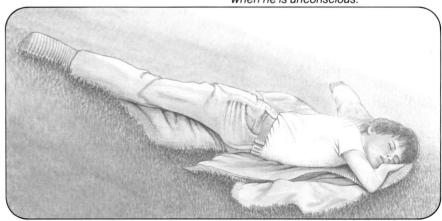

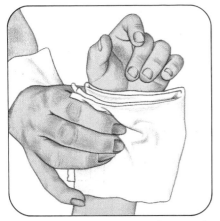

Place a gauze and lint dressing or a clean handkerchief on the wound. Press the wound with your fingers.

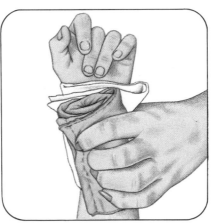

Place on the dressing something that is soft but provides effective pressure – e.g., a roll of bandage, or a rolled stocking or glove.

Wrap round a shawl, belt or sling. This must be knotted over the roll. Do not tie the bandage too tight. Take a look after a short time to make sure that the part of the body affected has not become cold.

What to do while the ambulance is on its way

- Make the child lie down. If he is unconscious, turn him on his side. Place his legs higher than his head, so that the blood will flow more quickly to his brain. Put a rug, an article of clothing or something similar under and over the child to stop him from getting cold.
- Give artificial respiration if necessary (see page 84).
- Staunch any bleeding with a suitable bandage.
- Make the child as comfortable as possible in order to ease the pain.
- Do not move an injured child unless it is absolutely necessary; his condition could be made worse.
- Never leave an injured child alone, because he is in great need of comfort and reassurance.
- Do not give a badly injured child anything to drink. He would be very likely to vomit, and swallowing could prove difficult.

If the child is conscious, let him lie on his back if he wants to do so, with his legs raised.

Poisoning

A surprising number of children suffer from poisoning at one time or another, especially at home or when visiting people who are not used to small children. The risk is greatest between the ages of one and three years, when children start to become curious about their surroundings and want to put everything in their mouths. Fortunately, most of these accidents do not end in tragedy, thanks to quick intervention or to the fact that not much of the poison has been swallowed. However, some children swallow sufficient poison to cause them long-term or even permanent damage.

With children most cases of poisoning occur because they eat or drink some poisonous substance, but they may also be due to the inhalation of noxious gases or to skin contact with something particularly harmful.

Medicines

Poisonous drugs can cause great harm. In contrast to many chemical preparations which produce immediate symptoms when they are taken, the effects of drugs may not appear until several hours have passed, by which time the condition of the child could be critical. If you discover what has happened in good time and take quick countermeasures the risk of serious injury will of course be reduced. Children are especially sensitive to certain medicines – e.g., to those containing iron, to those designed to treat allergies and to travel-sickness pills. Sleeping pills and tranquillizers can also cause very serious poisoning, even when taken in very small quantities. Pain-killers, like aspirin and

Aspro, which contain acetylsalicylic acid, can produce symptoms of poisoning even if the child has eaten no more than three or four tablets. Nose and ear drops can represent another hazard. Medicines are often stored in a place that is readily accessible to a child, such as an unlocked kitchen cabinet or on a table-top. A visitor carrying pills in her handbag may put it down carelessly, and when a child opens the bag and sees a tempting packet or tablets which look like sweets he may decide to do some tasting. Always hide your medicines well, and return old medicines to the chemists.

Chemicals

Cases of poisoning caused by chemicals occur frequently, and can have serious consequences. As long as these substances remain in the stomach they are relatively harmless, but when a child vomits or coughs there is a grave risk that something will enter the air-passages. Even a very small amount of such chemicals can (because of their low surface tension) spread over a wide area of the lungs, damaging them in the process. Examples of these products in general domestic use are petrol, liquid wax polish, methylated spirit and stain-remover. Even paint and cleaning fluids often contain these organic solvents. There are other substances which have a corrosive action and can seriously damage the gullet, and even endanger life. Examples of these are washing soda, ammonia, soldering flux, toilet-cleaners and detergents. Oven-cleaners, rust-

removers and metal polish can corrode the body too, and so can some of the fluids used in hobbies. Other preparations which it is best to keep hidden from little eyes and hands are setting and other hair-lotions. Setting lotions are particularly poisonous. Spirits in as small a quantity as two tablespoonfuls can seriously injure young children. Denatured alcohol (methylated spirit) can also do serious harm.

Stain-removers are usually extremely poisonous. The instructions and warnings on the bottle or carton should be read and heeded. Hide poisonous substances well out of reach. Do not keep any old bottles or tins containing chemical residues; let the paint shop, for example, have them. Do not pour them into the dustbin or down the lavatory pan.

Tobacco

The danger of poisoning from eating cigarettes has often been exaggerated, but if a child has swallowed more than half an inch (13mm) of a cigarette you must get him to vomit (see page 91). Tobacco juice, snuff and cigarette-ends soaked in water are more dangerous still.

All too often children think that pills and tablets are sweets.

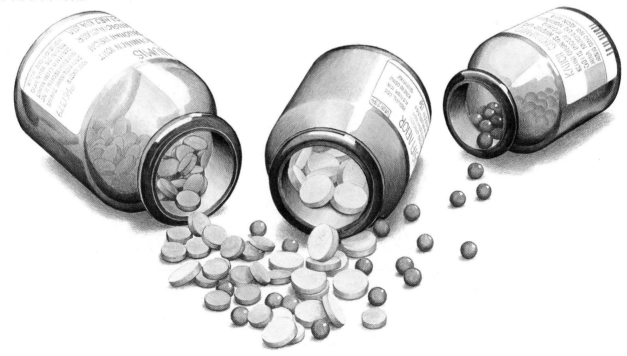

Poisonous plants

Often too much emphasis is placed on the danger of poisonous plants. Little children tend to eat such small amounts of plant material, whether poisonous or non-poisonous, that the problem is seldom serious. Furthermore, vomiting is usually one of the first symptoms of this type of poisoning.

However, this does not mean to say that you should not remove poisonous plants from your child's surroundings. *Laburnum* (golden chain), *mezereum*, *spurge olive*, *privet*, *yew*, *lily of the valley* and *spurge laurel* are examples of plants with berries or pods which look tempting to young children. Poisonous plants such as deadly nightshade (belladonna), henbane, Christmas rose, foxglove, broom, hemlock, oleander, larkspur and meadow saffron do not seem to interest children, and therefore very seldom cause accidents. Other plants such as the honey-locust and the common cow parsnip (or hog-weed) can produce considerable irritation of the skin, eyes and mucous membranes.

Laburnum
(Golden
Chain)

Lily of the valley

Spurge laurel

Poisonous mushrooms

Mushroom poisoning (harmless 'mushrooms' and poisonous 'toadstools' is a quite unreal distinction) can be very serious, and sometimes fatal. Never let your child go mushroom-picking without adult supervision. There are three mushrooms which are particularly deadly:

The Death Cap has caused a great number of deaths in Europe in recent years. It is often mistaken for an edible mushroom, so be very careful when picking white 'mushrooms', especially when they are young. Even when cooked, the poison remains as virulent as when they are raw.

On the other hand, the poison of the Lorchel (*Gyromitra esculenta*) is removed

Destroying Angel

Lorchel

Inocybe fastigiata   Death Cap

by boiling it for ten minutes (the water in which it has been boiled is poisonous, however, and must be thrown away). The Lorchel is found in conifer woods. Although, as has been said, this fungus can be made fit to eat by prolonged boiling, it is best avoided altogether, since cases are known where experienced gourmets have eventually been poisoned by it.

The Destroying Angel (*Amanita virosa*) is another example of a poisonous mushroom that has been responsible for many deaths. In addition to these very dangerous fungi, there are others which can make people ill without directly endangering their lives: for example, the Earthy Inocybe (*Inocybe geophylla*), the Sickener (*Russula emetica*), the Panther Cap (*Amanita pantherina*), which can be fatal and is sometimes mistaken for the edible Blusher (*Amanita rubescens*), *Inocybe fastigiata*, and the Fly Agaric (*Amanita muscaria*).

The treatment of poisoning

If your child has been poisoned you must act quickly. Never wait for the telltale symptoms. The longer the poison remains in the body, the more serious the damage will be.

If your child is still conscious after eating or drinking something poisonous

- Immediately give him 1 or 2 glasses of liquid, preferably milk, to drink; this will dilute the poison.
- Phone the doctor or the hospital (this is vital!). If you are advised to make the child vomit, proceed as follows:
- If the child is small you can tuck him under your arm, but in any case make sure his arms are securely pinioned. Bend him over a basin and then insert the index and middle finger of your right hand as far as you can into his gullet. Move your fingers (make sure that the nails are short) backward and forward inside his throat. In a minute or two he will begin to retch, but do not remove your hand until he is sick. If you are unsuccessful take the child to hospital.
- If the risk of poisoning is great, lose no time by trying to make the child vomit but take him to hospital.
- Make sure that the child drinks before you make him vomit, and after he has done so give him a preparation of activated charcoal.
- When the poison is a petroleum product the best thing to give is cream, ice-cream, milk, etc. These fatty fluids reduce the danger of vomiting, which might in this case cause lung damage. Take the child to the hospital.
- If the poison is *caustic*, immediately give the child plenty to drink, but do not give him so much that he starts to vomit, as that could cause further injury. Clean his skin if he has splashed himself and remove wet clothing. The same applies to petroleum products.

If a child has inhaled something poisonous

Give the child fresh air. It is most important for him to rest in a comfortable, half-sitting position. Get in touch with the doctor or the hospital.

Skin that has been in contact with harmful substances

Quickly rinse with water and then wash thoroughly with soap and water. If the poison has been splashed in the eyes, wash them with water for 10—15 minutes (see page 77). Phone the doctor.

General advice

- Keep the child under constant observation. Note any changes. If he stops breathing give artificial respiration straight away.
- Never give a semi-conscious child anything to drink and do not try to make him vomit. Just lay the child on his side (see page 83).
- Never make a child vomit when he has swallowed a caustic substance or a petroleum product.

Dangers in the world of the child

All children have a right to safety, especially in the places where they live. While modern technology has certainly made life easier, it has made the world a more dangerous place for the young. The notes that follow are reminders of some of the situations which are dangerous for children of different ages.

In babies there is a great risk of *injury from falls*.

- Never leave your baby lying on a bed or sofa, even with pillows or cushions round him.
- The sides of the child's cot must be at least 18 inches (nearly half a metre) high and the distance between the bars must be no more than 2¾ inches (70mm). Make sure that the bottom and drop-side are secure.
- Put safety locks on windows and balcony doors.
- Remove anything which a child might climb on from balconies and verandas.
- Fence off stairs or dangerous doorways.
- Make sure that bookcases and other pieces of furniture cannot topple over when a child climbs on them.
- Put a solid-based stool which will not tip in the bathroom, and make sure that the stair-carpet is not loose.

An electric shock can cause serious injury.

- Disconnect domestic appliances and put them out of the reach of children.
- All electric points must be child-proof.
- Make sure that light sockets always have bulbs in them.
- Check that each piece of electrical equipment in the home is covered by a safety guarantee and is not damaged.

Burns are typical hazards for toddlers when they start exploring the house and garden. However, much can be done to prevent them.

- Do not sit the child on your lap when you are having a hot drink.
- Test the child's food to make sure it is not too hot.
- Always put cold water in tubs and buckets before adding hot. This rule applies to the child's bath.
- Never leave children alone in the bathroom.
- Point pan-handles towards the back of stoves.
- Place a guard in front of open fires and hot stoves.
- Make sure that stoves and heaters cannot be tipped over.
- Central-heating radiators which are too hot are liable to cause burns. Turn the thermostat down.
- Always keep irons out of the reach of children.
- Be very careful with inflammable liquids such as paraffin and petrol. Store them in a safe place and do not let children play with the cans. It is best not to keep strong acids or alkalis in the house.

Little children do not realize they might fall if they lean out of a window. Neither do they realize how far away the ground is! All windows must have safety locks.

A child may use a table-cloth to pull herself up, but she can easily yank a cup of hot tea or a heavy ash-tray on top of herself.

Children are extremely inquisitive and will readily poke pins, scissors and knitting needles into electric sockets.

Be careful a child does not pinch his fingers in doors.

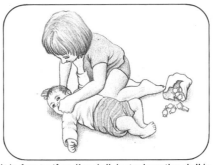

It is fun to 'feed' a doll, but when the doll is a live baby, the baby's life can be at stake.

It is exciting to look inside a plastic bag. How can a child of this age know that she will suffocate if the plastic clings to her nose and mouth?

The kitchen is no place for a child to play. An accident such as this is completely unnecessary. Guards are on sale for stoves and ovens.

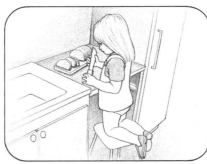

When you are as small as this little girl scissors, knives and other dangerous cutlery must be kept out of your reach,

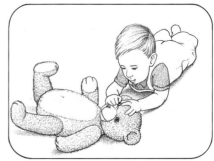

Children like to pull bits and pieces off their toys and put them in their mouths. This teddy-bear's eye was not properly secured.

A cot with bars must be protected round the sides (with material. say) so that a child cannot get stuck in them. Tie blind-cords out of children's way.

Flames are attractive, and unfortunately many children are burnt by them. Teach your child to be careful with fire, and keep matches out of reach.

It is nice to be able to do things for your-self, but if you are small and things are out of reach accidents can happen. Bathroom stools must not be liable to tip over.

Suffocation is a danger to children of any age.

- Never put a baby in harness or strings which might slip round his neck. Never put plastic sheets in any bed; rubber, mackintosh ones are safer as mattress protectors.
- Baby's pillow must not be too soft.
- Children under the age of three years often put things in their mouths, so never give them toys they can pull to pieces. Rattles and other toys may contain small balls of lead or plastic which can choke a child.
- Dolls and toy animals stuffed with pieces of polyester are dangerous when the seams split and the filling comes out. If a child tries to swallow a piece it could block his windpipe.
- Toys made of hard plastic break easily and can cause cuts. Examples of dangerous plastic toys are dolls' tea-sets, toy feeding bottles and dummies and rattles.
- Remove the pips from oranges, and never give peanuts to small children.
- A dummy must be made in such a way that it is impossible for the child to stuff it completely into his mouth, and he must not be able to suck the teat loose.
- Do not leave a child alone in bed with his feeding-bottle.

Drowning can happen at home as well as out-of-doors.

- Never leave small children in the bath by themselves or near tubs or pails full of water.
- Pits filled with water, ponds and ditches are a drowning hazard.
- Wells and rainwater-barrels must be securely covered to prevent little children falling into them.
- Fence in swimming pools to stop children going too near them.
- Flippers, diving goggles and snorkels must be used only by good swimmers and certainly not by children under the age of twelve. A snorkel must not be longer than 10 inches (250mm) to make it easy for the child to breathe out and to draw fresh air.
- When children go sledging in winter their heads must be well protected. Do not let your child slide down a hill which ends in a busy street or has a wall or hedge at the bottom. Bales of straw can also be dangerous in winter when they freeze hard.
- Protect the knees, elbows and seat of a child who is learning to skate. Stuff foam plastic under his clothes. Make sure that the child has guards on his skates when he is carrying them, and that he has no skates on his feet on the way to and from the ice-rink.
- Give the child a riding hat to wear when he goes horse-riding. This hard helmet must be firmly fixed so as not to drop off if the child has a fall. Do not let a child go out riding by himself too soon. Most accidents occur when children are unaccompanied.
- Show children the proper way to treat animals. A horse, dog or cat can become frightened and kick, bite or scratch in self-defence.

Children can drown in pits with a low water-level, such as those found on build-ing sites. Small children cannot read notice boards.

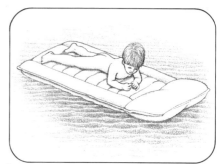

An air-bed should never be used on the water. It can easily drift out to sea.

It is fun to climb on log piles or on stacks of cement pipes, but the logs or pipes can roll over on top of a child.

If a child is playing or fishing at the water's edge it is best for him to wear a life-jacket. It goes without saying that he must wear one in a boat or on a jetty.

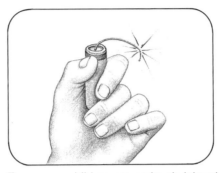

Every year children are seriously injured by explosives. Be very careful with fireworks and do not let children pick up any objects at shooting ranges.

Darts, bows and arrows, air-guns and catapults are dangerous toys which can cause serious eye injuries.

Children enjoy climbing trees but the game can go badly wrong if a hood, scarf or jacket-cord becomes entangled in a branch.

This seesaw is dangerous and should be adjusted so that it does not come down too hard or squash the children's feet.

A sledge must be fitted with a seat so that the child can sit on it with knees bent. The hands must be kept in the sledge.

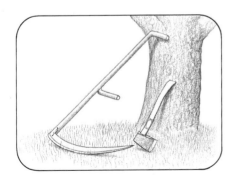

Children love exploring their surroundings, so try to remove the dangers that might be waiting for them. Hide sharp tools and dangerous chemicals.

When playing ice hockey, a child needs to wear a helmet to protect his head.

Warn children not to walk on thin or broken ice.

Children in traffic

Accidents are often caused by children running across the street.

Reports on the causes of traffic accidents involving children reveal that we are not sufficiently aware of the limited extent to which they can look after themselves in traffic. We know very little about how children experience the changes in the traffic situation from moment to moment. Many adults, too, fail to foresee possible dangers. As soon as we take children out we should remember that *anything can happen*. A child whose hand is not being held can suddenly run in front of a car because he has seen something interesting on the other side of the street. He can also run out for no apparent reason.

A risky place in which to play.

Children as pedestrians

When you are walking with your child along the pavement or by the side of the road, keep as close to him as possible so that you can grab him quickly. Of course, it is best to keep hold of the child's hand. Make a point of walking on the outside of the child, nearest the traffic, so that you can head him off if he makes a sudden movement. A child will sometimes lag behind because he is tired or because something has attracted his attention. Take care that he never stays out of arm's reach, and that your weariness or irritation does not get the better of you. In such cases it is best to pick the child up and carry him or to stop walking for a while to give him a breather. Do not let children play on the edge of the pavement. It is very difficult to foresee the situation which can cause accidents. For instance, a child who is swinging round a lamp-post may let go just as a car is coming along and be slung in front of it. Never stand on the edge of railway platforms whether you are with a child or on your own, and always make sure you are free to step backward; you do not want to be thrown against or under an incoming train as the crowd surges forward to meet it.

Children on bicycles

Children are just as unpredictable in traffic when they are riding bicycles. They could suddenly change direction if they spied something on the ground that they wanted to pick up. A child lives in a world of his own, and does not have an adult's ability to predict what the traffic will do.

He is too busy playing to notice a car.

Children can appear on the scene anywhere.

Accidents often happen because a car driver blows his horn when coming up behind a group of children on bicycles. The driver only wants to pass, but the children can be so startled that they start swaying and, in trying to move out of the way, can end up under the wheels of the car.

No child under the age of twelve years should go cycling in traffic. Research has shown that they do not have a sufficiently developed ability to assess traffic situa-

tions. It is also important not to give children bicycles which are too big, because they can fall off them fairly easily and suffer head injuries.

Children and cars

As a car driver, the expression 'right of way' is one you have to forget. As soon as you think that there may be children about, make sure you can pull up at a moment's notice. If you see a group of children just across the street and another child, who might be a friend, is standing on the opposite pavement, do not assume that the situation is under control, even though the child is looking in your direction. The child could dash out in front of you because he wants to show off, or simply because he does not want to be left behind.

A child who comes running out of a clump of trees is hardly ever alone – he is usually followed by other children who are less aware of the traffic than he is. Children are not able to take in the traffic situation at one glance, or to react to it adequately. Children regard zebra crossings as safe places where nothing can happen; instead of being extra careful, they are even less careful than at other times. Some 15 per cent of accidents in-

A car suddenly backs out . . .

volving children occur on zebra crossings.

A loud blast on the horn is more likely to frighten a child into doing something silly than to warn him to be careful. It is better not to hoot; instead slow down and get ready to make an emergency stop. If there is a child with you in the car, it is important to park the car on the right side of the street, so that you do not have to cross the road when you leave the car. This is especially true when you draw up near your own house. Many accidents have occurred because children have jumped out of a car and run across the road to get home quickly. This sort of accident can happen in the few seconds it takes you to lock the car. We should take advantage of walks and cycle trips with our children to teach them what happens in traffic.

Children think that zebra crossings are always safe.

The healthy child

For anyone who has to look after children, it is important to know that each child develops at his own rate. There are many factors – such as heredity, environment and physical health – which play a part in this. One child starts to walk when he is ten months, whereas another may not do so until he is one and a half years old or more. Such differences can be seen within a single family, so you must not attach too much importance to the fact that your child is not quite average in development.

However, it is important to record the differences, so that the child can be given timely help if this is needed. Perhaps the following simple guidelines will help you.

During the first few weeks a child spends most of his time resting. He eats, sleeps and cries. He has the reflexes of a newborn infant: he automatically grips your finger, makes sucking movements when his lips are touched and cringes when you touch the sole of his foot. He already reacts to noises. When a child is **6–8 weeks** old he begins to raise his head when lying on his tummy, and begins to follow a moving object with his eyes. The first smile usually appears around this time.

When a child is **3–4 months** old, he starts to gain more control over his movements. He can hold his head up straight and can roll over on to his back from his side. He also starts to chortle and to seize objects. He slowly learns to follow the movements of his hands and feet with his eyes, and turns his head in the direction of a sound.

When a child is **6 months** old he becomes increasingly inquisitive about his surroundings. He now rolls over from his back on to his tummy, and can sit up straight for short periods with a little support. He can transfer an object from one hand to the other. He now begins to recognize the person who is looking after him and enjoys companionship.

At **7–8 months** a child starts to crawl and can sit without support. He begins to react negatively to strange faces. This is the time when some children say their first word.

When a child is **9–10 months** old he stands with some support and walks by holding on to the furniture. He also begins to understand single simple words, and he can play peep-bo (or peek-a-boo) and wave back at you.

At **one year** some children start to walk on their own, but it is not unusual for others to be six months older before they can do so. The child can now manage to hold objects between his thumb and index finger. He starts to become proficient in using single words like Mum, look, car. At this age some children start feeding themselves. They begin to appreciate the notions of time and space.

When a child is **eighteen months to two years** old his powers of speech gradually develop, and he puts together his first short sentences. Some children are dry now during the day, but it is quite normal for this to happen later. A child will now help you dress him and is very good at feeding himself.

At **three years** a child enjoys his own interests and wants to do what pleases him rather than what his parents tell him to do; this is the period of protest, and he often comes into conflict with other children. He can now usually dress without help.

At **four years** most children can cut with scissors and can do simple drawings. They also have good muscular control. This is shown by the way that they can keep their balance on a small plank, and can build complicated structures with toy bricks, etc. They are better at telling colours apart.

Height and weight

Graphs such as those given on the next page are often used nowadays by health centres, clinics and school nurses. They are used mainly for discovering illnesses associated with emaciation or retarded growth.

However, the figures for length and weight have no more than a limited value, since each individual has his own constitution – i.e., has a natural tendency to be long, short, lean or well-built. Notice should be taken only of marked variations. But if a child is above average at the age of two and a half, he should not be below average at the age of three. Roughly 95 per cent of children have statistics lying between the upper and lower limits on the graphs.

The information in the graphs opposite is based on information from: Common Symptoms of Disease in Children by R. S. Illingworth (Blackwell Scientific Publications, 6th ed., 1979) and Standard from Birth to Maturity for Height, Weight, Height Velocity and Weight Velocity by J. M. Tanner, R. H. Whitehouse, M. Takaishi (Arch. Dis. Child., 41, 613, 1966).

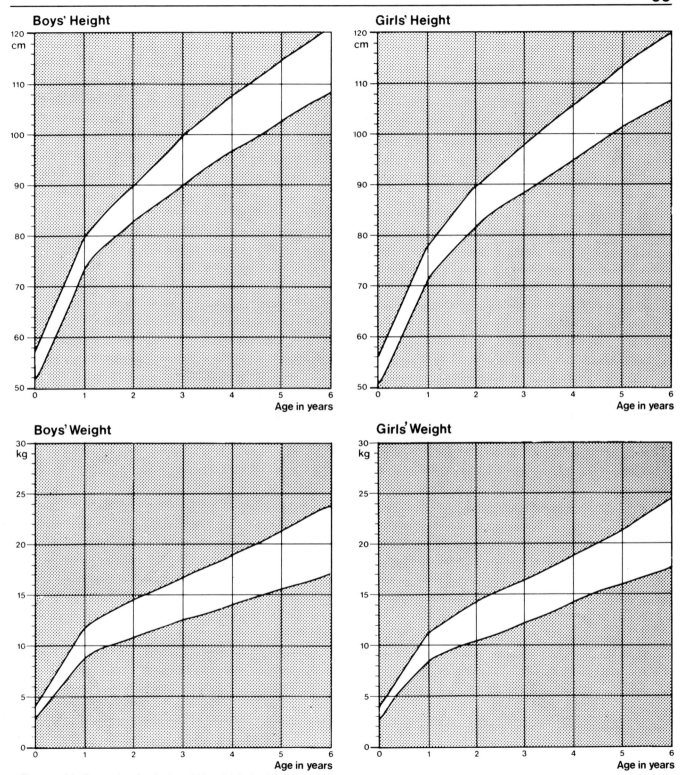

Boys' Height

Girls' Height

Boys' Weight

Girls' Weight

The outside lines give the limits within which the height and weight of the British child can vary at different ages. In recent years British children have been rather taller and heavier.

Correct feeding

It is important for everyone to eat well. But for children it is especially important because a proper diet helps both their physical and their mental development. We eat to obtain energy. Excess energy, or 'fuel', is stored in the body as fat and we put on weight. Proteins, fats and carbohydrates are foods which give us energy. The body also requires a number of other materials such as minerals, vitamins and water, in order to be able to function. The materials help the body to process the energy supply.

Proteins

Proteins are the building bricks of the body, and are particularly significant for growing children in whom so much new cell-formation is going on. Proteins consist of amino acids, and some of them are essential to life. They are chiefly found in animal foodstuffs such as fish, meat, milk and dairy produce. Because proteins are not stored in the body, they have to be consumed daily.

Fats

Fat supplies energy – weight for weight twice as much as is supplied by proteins and carbohydrates. Fat is composed of various kinds of saturated and unsaturated fatty acids. One of the unsaturated fatty acids is linoleic acid. This cannot be made by the body, yet it is very important because it holds down the level of cholesterol in the blood. Linoleic acid is abundant in maizegerm oil, sunflower oil and soya oil, and is present to a lesser extent in margarine, whereas milk fat and coconut oil are low in fatty acids. A hot oven can convert unsaturated fatty acids into saturated fatty acids.

Carbohydrates

Sugar, starch and cellulose are different sorts of carbohydrate. Carbohydrates serve mainly as suppliers of energy. Sugar is the most ready source of energy, and is useful in situations requiring prolonged physical exertion; on the other hand, it contains none of the necessary foodstuffs. It is popularly said to contain 'free' calories. However, it can prove harmful to the teeth. Starch, which is found in bread, in cereals and in vegetables, especially in tubers, is the most important and most useful source of carbohydrates.

Cellulose, an essential constituent of all plants, is indigestible by man but very important, because the fibres stimulate peristalsis (bowel activity) and help to prevent constipation.

Minerals

Minerals do not supply energy, but they do perform other important functions. Calcium and phosphorus are necessary for the development of the bones and teeth, and iron for the manufacture of red blood corpuscles. Iron is contained in, among other things, liver, liver pâté, meat, black pudding, spinach and green cabbage. The body finds it easier to make full use of the iron if something containing vitamin C (citrus fruits, fresh green vegetables – provided they are not overcooked) is eaten at the same time.

Vitamins

Most normal foods contain traces of vitamins. If a child eats a fairly wide range of food, he will obtain all the vitamins he needs, but children under school age must be given extra doses of vitamins A and D.

Water

The body is 70 per cent water. An adult loses about 3½ pints (2 litres) of water per day and must therefore replace the same quantity. We do this mainly by drinking, but even our food contains much water. Remember that both adults and children need to drink more on hot days.

Fibres

Fibres are indigestible parts of certain foodstuffs and are found in greens, wholemeal bread, muesli and unrefined cereal products. Because the body is unable to break down the fibres, they provide 'roughage' and tend to prevent constipation. They are also useful because they can make the stomach feel pleasantly 'full' without overloading the body with excess fat and protein.

Energy

The food we eat is oxidized in the body and supplies the necessary energy to keep it in operation. The amount of energy delivered varies greatly from foodstuff to foodstuff. Until a short time ago the quantity of energy supplied by proteins, fats and carbohydrates was measured in calories. Nowadays dieticians have switched to the international unit of energy known as the joule (J). One kilocalorie (kcal) is equivalent to 4·2 kilojoules (kJ).

Proteins are found in fish, meat, eggs, milk, cheese etc.

Proteins are important for growing children, who have intense cell-production

Proteins are necessary for the cell-replacement that constantly occurs. Most cells are replaced continuously.

During a single year practically our whole body disappears, to be replaced by a new one.

The proteins which are not used for cell-building are converted into energy.

Fats
Our bodies also need fat. Part of the intake has to be unsaturated fat. Margarine is one of the foods which supplies this.

Fat supplies twice the amount of energy supplied by proteins and carbohydrates.

Oxidation provides energy for movement, thinking and other activities.

Anyone who is physically active needs plenty of energy.

Carbohydrates are the best sources of energy; in particular, the starch found in cereals, flour and vegetables supplies a large amount of energy.

Carbohydrates
Starch, sugar and cellulose are varieties of carbohydrate.

Starch
is found in flour, cereals and vegetables, especially in tubers.

Sugar
does not contain essential foodstuffs, but rapidly enters the bloodstream and so can supply quick short-term energy for physical effort.

Energy supply/time

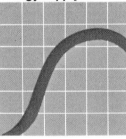

Vitamins
are required by the body so that it can, among other things, take proper advantage of the other foodstuffs.

Minerals
are needed to help the body function correctly. The most important are calcium, phosphorus and iron.

Cellulose
is found in all plants. Humans cannot digest it, but it plays an important part in the activity of the intestines.

Water
Our bodies are 70% water. Some 2–3½ pints (approx. 1–2 litres) disappear daily and have to be replaced from the food and drink.

Eat a varied diet but not too much

Important as it is that children eat a varied diet – i.e., something from each of the four groups on our 'food-tray' – it is equally important that they do not overeat. Take care that a child does not sow the seeds of a lifetime of trouble by becoming fat.

Weighing a child is the simplest way of discovering whether or not he is over-weight or underweight. If he weighs more than normal, it is time to give him a little less to eat. However, make sure that his diet remains varied; do not cut out any item, but give him slightly less of everything.

The right food at the right time

It is important for a child to eat at regular times. Breakfast should provide a good foundation and should contain 20 to 25 per cent of the daily food requirements. Lunch and dinner (or dinner and high tea as the case may be) should each contain around 30 per cent of the daily food re-quirements, and lighter meals or snacks not more than 15 to 20 per cent. However, if a child really cannot face food early in the morning do not force him to eat. Try instead to make sure he has a milky drink, and takes some fruit and cheese to eat mid-morning at school.

The specimen food tray

We constantly hear it said that we eat too much protein and too many fats; on the other hand, slimming diets have banned the so-called 'fattening foods' such as bread, potatoes and peas and beans.

The food tray in the diagram gives us a guide to the proportions of different types of food we should eat. It encourages us to use more brown bread, potatoes, legu-minous plants (e.g., peas, different types of beans), vegetables and fresh fruit, and less meat and dairy produce.

The food-tray

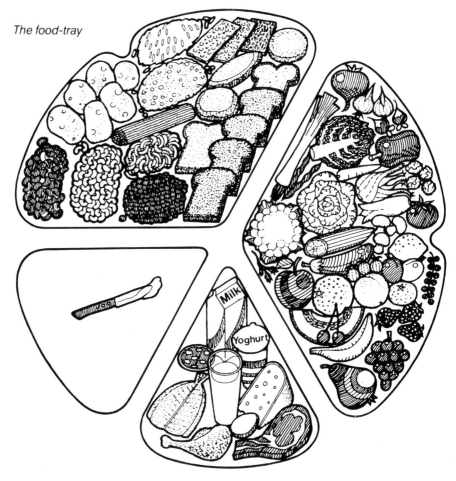

Points to remember

- Be careful with sugar, which supplies 'free' calories – i.e., energy without nutrition. It is also bad for the teeth. There is absolutely no need to put sugar in tea or coffee or yoghurt. A single lump of sugar contains 20 kcal. and four lumps of sugar per day amount to 6–7 lb of fatty tissue in a year.
- Avoid superfluous fat. Trim all visible fat from meat. Switch to a margarine labelled 'high in polyunsaturates' and spread it thinly on your bread, leaving it off altogether with meat paste or cream cheese.
- Fats are used in cooking too, so fry in corn oil or sunflower oil – these oils are composed mainly of unsaturated fatty acids.
- Use milk or skimmed milk instead of cream in tea and coffee. Do not add butter to potatoes and other vegetables and keep the whipped cream for festive occasions.
- Milk can be consumed in various forms: for example yoghurt or cheese. Porridge is made with milk. Use half-cream milk, or skimmed milk – it is less fattening than full-cream milk.
- Bread and potatoes will not make you fat – provided you do not spread too much butter on your bread, do not mash the potatoes with butter or fry them!
- Bread can be replaced by cereals or farinaceous foods. If you eat porridge or pancakes, you must reduce the amount of bread you consume. It is better to eat wholemeal bread and bran crisp bread.
- Chewing is good for you. Your teeth need the exercise – so eat wholewheat bread, fresh fruit and raw vegetables.

A few suggestions for a good breakfast

Breakfast with porridge

a small bowl of porridge
wholewheat toast or bread
with peanut butter
cheese
apple

Breakfast with yoghurt

low-fat natural yoghurt with plenty of fresh, chopped fruit
wholewheat toast or bread
with Marmite or cottage cheese

Breakfast with egg

boiled or poached egg
wholewheat toast or bread
fruit juice or an orange

Breakfast with bacon

grilled lean bacon
grilled tomato
wholemeal toast or bread
fruit juice

These menus can of course be varied. The important point to remember is that a good breakfast should provide energy, protein, vitamins and minerals. It should be low in fats – so avoid fried foods, and spread margarine thinly, or spread cottage cheese or peanut butter directly on to wholewheat bread or toast. It should also be low in sugar, so avoid jams and marmalades (try Marmite, cottage cheese or peanut butter instead) and pre-sweetened, refined breakfast cereals.

The sick child in hospital

At first sight, all the equipment in a hospital can look daunting. If your child has to be admitted to hospital, you can show him the following photographs to give him some idea of what will happen.

Jenny has an earache. By using a head-reflector, the doctor can look deep into her auditory canal in order to discover the precise location of the inflammation (the cause of the pain). The round, concave mirror partly covers his face, in order to

reflect as brightly as possible the light coming from a lamp placed at an angle behind Jenny's mother. The beam of light is thrown straight down the long auditory canal and the doctor looks along its path through a small round hole in the mirror.

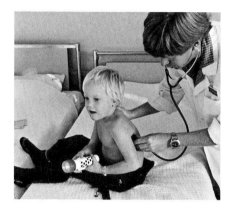

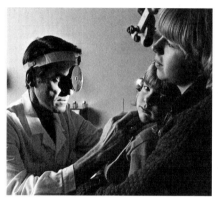

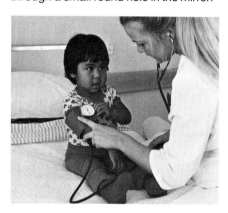

Here the doctor is sounding Jim's chest with a stethoscope. The 'cup' he is placing on different parts of the child's back and chest picks up the sound made by the lungs as Jim breathes in and out or when he coughs. The sounds picked up by the cup of the instrument are transmitted via the tube to the doctor's ears. By using the stethoscope, he can hear if the cough comes from the trachea (the windpipe) and if Jim's cold is accompanied by a lung infection. He can also hear how well the heart is working when he places the cup on the left side of the chest.

reflect as brightly as possible the light coming from a lamp placed at an angle behind Jenny's mother. The beam of light is thrown straight down the long auditory canal and the doctor looks along its path through a small round hole in the mirror.

Eventually the flow of blood is cut off, and Mary then releases some air until she can hear the blood flowing again and she reads the blood pressure on the white dial.

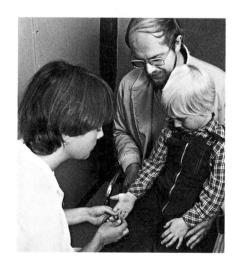

Many children, and adults too, are nervous about having a blood sample taken by a prick on the finger. It would be silly to say it does not hurt, but it is no worse than a gnat bite. It can even be interesting to watch the nurse collect the drops of blood in a small glass tube placed against the finger-tip.

John is in the radiography department (right), having a picture taken of the insides of his body. This is done with a special camera that emits an invisible light known as 'X-rays'. Although we cannot see the images made by this light, they show up on a photographic plate. John may have swallowed a coin and, if so, the photograph will show exactly where it is in his alimentary canal. The camera has been set up to take a picture of the interior of John's chest. If you look carefully, you will see a silhouette like a window-pane on his skin. This is so that the camera can be pointed at the right place.

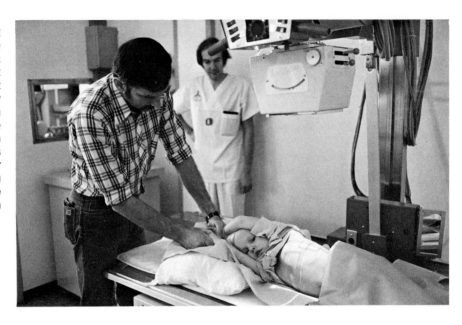

In the picture below, the action of Eric's heart is being studied. In this test the extremely weak electrical impulses of a beating heart are measured. The apparatus records these impulses as a zigzag line traced on a roll of chart paper. The examination is called an ECG, which is short for electrocardiogram; this simply means '*Electrical Cardiac* (or heart) impulse *Graph*'. The technician places small contact discs in a certain pattern on Eric's chest. These discs have wires running from them to a measuring instrument that detects the extremely weak electrical impulses emitted by the heart. Eric himself feels nothing, however, as the instrument does not hurt him at all.

Sarah is seen here in the play-room. This is where children go after meals and the daily tests, if they are well enough. Many children in hospital do not need to lie in bed all day; instead they can draw and paint, or sew or do carpentry, or just sit and read.

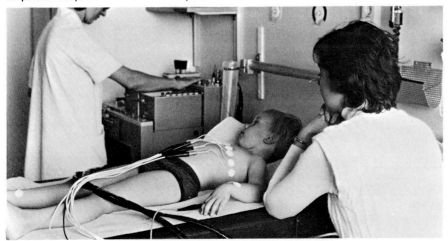

The sick child at home

Most children fall ill a few times during a year. Generally the trouble is a cold, ear-ache, stomach-ache or one of the common infectious diseases of childhood. Parents are always anxious the first few times a child falls ill, but they quickly learn the child's individual rhythm and can tell soon enough that something is wrong. They learn to judge the symptoms and to tell how seriously to take them. The morning is a good time for assessing a child's state of health. A healthy child behaves in much the same way as usual when he wakes; a sick child is tired and listless, unusually quiet or unusually irritable.

Staying in bed

When a child is so ill that he ought to stay in bed he will do so voluntarily nine times out of ten. However, he may prefer to lie in your bed or on a sofa somewhere where he can be near you. Cool sheets are soothing to a child who has a fever, but avoid piling too many blankets on top of him or dressing him in very thick clothes. If a child is dressed too warmly, his temperature can rise still further.

If the child does not to want to stay in bed, it is better to let him get up and play a little than to force him to lie in bed. Try to keep his play quiet and persuade him to have a rest every so often.

The better a child feels, the more inventive you have to be to keep him occupied. Keep a box of bits and pieces containing, for example, toys the child has stopped playing with for some time. You can also put in several small books, Plasticine, coloured crayons, paper, a pair of blunt scissors, pieces of material etc. – in other words, all the things which will keep a child amused for hours at a time.

When a child is up and about again

When a child is better he will want to be up and about again, and this will be best for him unless the doctor says otherwise, and provided he does not overtire himself. At the same time, the fact that a child is well enough to get up and play does not necessarily mean that he is well enough to play with his friends or his brothers and sisters. When a child has been suffering from a serious or prolonged illness – pneumonia, say, or a severe bout of measles – it is preferable to keep him indoors for a day or two after his tempera-ture has returned to normal. In certain diseases such as whooping-cough, fresh air is very beneficial. Here again, however, playing with friends could tax the child's strength. There is also the risk of spreading the infection. Some of the other children could have diseases which would make even the common infectious diseases potentially fatal.

School or day nursery can be too tiring for a convalescent child, so it is best to keep him at home.

Liquids are more important than solid food

Feverish children seldom feel hungry. Do not make them eat; their appetites will return when they start to recover. If the illness is prolonged, give the child small portions of his favourite food. Porridge is good, because it contains plenty of nourishment. Most children like ice-cream even when they are unwell; it is also quite nutritious, as is fruit.

However, the most important thing is for the child to take in sufficient liquid, especially when he is running a high tem-perature and perspiring or when he is suffering from an attack of vomiting and diarrhoea. If the liquid is not replaced, there is a risk of dehydration. A feverish child should drink 1¼ to 1¾ pints per day, and more if he has diarrhoea, vomiting attacks, or is perspiring, or if he is short of breath. It is easier to make sure bottle-fed infants are taking enough liquid than it is to make sure that bigger children are. Try to tempt older children with different drinks such as orange juice, milk, water or cocoa.

Make the patient as comfortable as possible. Put a good-sized table next to the bed for his toys, books etc. A table for the bed, as shown in the photo, can easily be made from a cardboard box with a crescent-shaped piece cut out each side. A box like this is stable enough for the child to do a puzzle on it or make a model. A basket fastened to the bed is handy for used paper handkerchiefs or other rubbish.

The family medicine cabinet

Useful medicines to keep in the house

- Tablets for feverishness and pain such as aspirin-based remedies.
- Cough medicines as recommended by the doctor or chemist. These include an expectorant for dry coughs and something to loosen tenacious phlegm.
- Medicines for diarrhoea or preparations containing activated charcoal which can be given in certain cases of poisoning.
- An ointment or lotion to soothe itching and smarting – e.g., zinc ointment or calamine lotion.
- Petroleum jelly or other recommended ointment for sore buttocks in babies.

- A skin cream for chapped hands, dry skin and scratches.
- Sunburn cream.
- Nose drops (only as prescribed by the doctor).

  Keep all medicines out of the reach of children. It is important to make sure that they do not become damp, so do not store them in the bathroom. Some medicines have to be kept cold, so it might be worthwhile buying a small lockable box which can be put in the refrigerator.

Use medicines correctly

Always follow the exact instructions for use issued with the medicines, whether they are obtained on prescription or not. Improper use can do a great deal of harm. Medicines have a limited shelf life. Check the date stamp or ask the chemist. Never keep any that are out of date or left over from a course of treatment – return them to the shop.

Handy bandaging materials for domestic use

Wound cleaners (lint impregnated with a wound-cleansing agent)

Lint

Wadding

Netelast

Tubegauz (with applicator)

Adhesive plasters (stretchy) with dressings

Waterproof plasters with dressings

Rolls of adhesive plaster (available in different widths but without wound dressings)

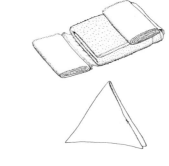

Slings

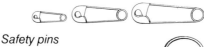

Safety pins

Scissors

Tweezers (pointed and blunt)

Thermometer

On excursions

If you are taking children out on a trip, equip yourself with a waterproof bag containing the following items:
- Wound cleaners
- Adhesive plasters with dressings
- Crêpe bandage
- Slings
- A roll of adhesive plaster

Give the right amount

Try to give your child his medicines at set times. Never increase or reduce the dose without consulting the doctor.

Never give one child medicine prescribed for another.

Tablets and capsules

These have to be taken via the mouth. Some have to be swallowed whole because, for example, they taste nasty or can attack the teeth. Some medicines are intended to act over a period of time and are contained in capsules which release their contents slowly into the stomach or intestines. If your child has difficulty in swallowing tablets, ask the doctor to prescribe the liquid equivalent if possible. Tablets which may be crushed can be mixed with a piece of fruit or with fruit juice, but do not mix them with the bottle feed or with the ordinary meal. However, be careful over concealing tablets in food because a child can take a permanent dislike to anything used as a vehicle for a nasty-tasting medicine.

Liquid medicines

Nowadays these are measured in millilitres (ml). In order to gauge the correct quantity of medicine, place the spoon on the table. Domestic teaspoons vary too much in size to be safe; always use the special plastic one supplied by the chemist.

Some liquid medicines settle into layers, so shake them well before pouring.

Drops

It is important that the correct number of drops are applied to the right place.

Eye-drops. Bend the child's head back. Pull the lower lid down and let the drops fall between the eye and the eyelid. Do not touch the eye or the eyelashes. Close the eye and let the child blink.

Nose-drops. Get the child to blow his nose, and then lay him on his back with his head bent well back. Put the drops in both nostrils. Turn his head alternately to left and right.

Nasal spray. Make sure that the nose has been well blown. Then get the child to sit or stand (never let him lie down) with his head erect and insert the tip of the spray in one of the nostrils. Squeeze the bottle several times (as directed on the label). Never exceed the stated dose. Nasal sprays should definitely not be used on children under the age of ten.

Nose-drops or nasal sprays must not be used for longer than 10 consecutive days, otherwise the mucous membranes could become irritated. It is best to wait for 7–10 days before the preparation is used again.

Ear-drops. Lay the child on his side. Support your hand and make sure that the drops really enter his ear. Ear-drops are preferably employed at room temperature.

Remember that eye and ear drops often have a limited life.

Ointments

Skin ointment. Squeeze a small quantity from the tube on to a piece of lint or smear the lint with a little ointment from the pot. Do not use fingers. Then apply a thin layer of ointment to the skin.

Ointments for the nose, eyes or anus are packed in a tube with a long nozzle. Eye ointment emerges from the tube as a thin ribbon, and as with the drops, should be introduced under the lower lid.

Ointment for the anus is best applied when the child is lying on his side with his knees drawn up or when he is kneeling on all fours.

Child health care

The child-health clinic

This country has a good reputation for child care, which starts with the post-natal check-up. It is not obligatory to visit child-health clinics, but most parents are glad to avail themselves of their services.

Clinics vary in the way they are run but have the same overall aim – to provide qualified physical and mental care for children during the first years of life.

A few days after birth (or after mother and child have left the maternity ward) a midwife or health visitor will usually call to take a look at the child and give advice. If the mother is fit enough she can visit the clinic herself in a week or two. There the baby will be weighed and measured and given a medical examination by the doctor; advice will also be offered on feeding. From then on the baby can be taken to the clinic every week or two, or whenever necessary. At six weeks the doctor will examine the child again, paying particular attention to his heart, lungs, lymphatic glands, abdominal organs, sex organs, eyes and hips. His movements, reflexes and sense-organs will also be checked.

When a baby is healthy, and is developing normally, the clinic will give him a series of injections, starting at three months, with the parents' consent (see page 112).

Other options are discussion groups involving parents and medical personnel. These groups are often led by a child psychologist, who will give advice on such matters as sleeping problems, anorexia nervosa, etc.

Testing sight and hearing

Clinics test a child's hearing when he is between the ages of 9 and 13 months. His hearing is tested for high and low notes. If the child squints he will be referred to the oculist.

The examination of one-year-olds

At one year, children are given a thorough medical examination involving both their physical and their mental health.

Tests on one- to three-year-olds

These include examinations of physical fitness, vision, hearing, speech, development and behaviour. Parents can take time to describe their child's mental and social development, the quality of the relationship between them and the child, how well he eats and sleeps, whether he is clean or not, whether or not he is nervous or jealous, and how he gets on with other children, etc. The clinic will try to help parents with any problems. In some cases, psychological assistance will be required, in others the social services may be able to do what is necessary.

Children in day nurseries

When a child is brought to a clinic from a day nursery, it is best if he is accompanied by a parent or by someone from the nursery who can say what is wrong with him, and can be given information and advice. If it is the parents who take the child to the clinic, they and the medical adviser there can report to the staff at the nursery later. Day nurseries receive regular visits from the health authorities.

School health care

When a child starts school the school has a degree of responsibility for his health. A summary of the child's clinic health record will be passed to the school medical officer by the child-health clinic.

Inoculation

Testing the child's sight at the clinic.

What is inoculation?

When bacteria or viruses invade the body and cause an infectious disease antibodies are produced. In vaccination bacteria or viruses are supplied to the body in attenuated or 'killed' form. The body then forms antibodies exactly as if the individual had contracted the disease, so that when he or she is subsequently exposed to the germs the antibodies needed to deal with them are already in the blood-stream. Most vaccines do not give permanent immunity, so the treatment has to be repeated at intervals.

What is gamma globulin?

Gamma globulin is made from human blood and contains a number of antibodies. Among other things, it protects against measles and jaundice and is administered before or just after the infection. The protection lasts only as long as the antibodies remain in the body – i.e., for 3–4 weeks. However, the protection against jaundice lasts longer than this.

Inoculation of a child who is already infected

It is too late to think about inoculations when the child has already been infected, but when a small or weak child has measles, for instance, it is important to give him gamma globulin. This can lighten the course of the disease or prevent it from breaking out. In all inoculations it is essential for the child to be healthy when he is inoculated. Even a common cold can be a hindrance.

How are vaccinations carried out?

The injections are given in the buttocks, in the outside of the thigh or in the upper arm.

Diphtheria, tetanus and pertussis vaccine

This triple vaccine gives protection against diphtheria, tetanus and whooping-cough. The diphtheria and tetanus vaccines can be given together without the whooping-cough vaccine. The whooping-cough vaccine can be given on its own up to the age of 3.

Thanks to the general programme of inoculation, diphtheria has virtually died out in Britain, but the disease is present elsewhere – e.g., in Eastern Europe. The vaccine has no side-effects. Protecting a child against tetanus is very important, as tetanus bacteria – which are found among other things in sand and soil – can enter the body via deep wounds.

Because both the tetanus and diphtheria vaccines provide protection for only a number of years, children are given a diphtheria and tetanus booster at around the age of five years, when the child is due to start school.

The diphtheria, tetanus and pertussis vaccine is given three times: from 3 months old, at 5–6 months and at 9–11 months. The injections are usually given in the thigh or the upper arm, and the place is a little sore.

Polio

Thanks to widespread vaccination, polio has become rather rare. A child is given three doses of polio vaccine, by mouth, at the same time as the triple vaccine mentioned above. When he is about five years, he receives another dose of vaccine. The vaccine has no side-effects.

Measles

Children are inoculated against measles at 14 or 15 months. The vaccine is thought to give lifelong immunity.

About a third of the children who are vaccinated suffer from feverishness and a light rash approximately one week after the vaccination, but the trouble quickly subsides and they are not infectious.

Care must be taken with this vaccine in children who are oversensitive to eggs. The health clinic can advise here.

German measles

German measles is a mild and harmless disease in children, and there is no need to inoculate small children against it. Nevertheless, girls who have not had the disease should be inoculated against it with an eye to the future, because German measles is a hazard to unborn children during the first three months of pregnancy. This inoculation is usually given between the ages of 10 and 14 years. Make sure your daughter has this inoculation if there is any doubt as to whether or not she has had German measles.

The vaccine can cause a certain amount of joint pain, but this disappears within a few days. An inoculation against German measles offers very good protection throughout the child-bearing period of a woman's life.

Almette-Guérin vaccination for tuberculosis

The BCG vaccine for tuberculosis is usually given to boys and girls when they are about 13. Some parts of the United Kingdom offer the BCG vaccine to all new-born babies.

Smallpox

Vaccination for smallpox has now largely been abandoned because the disease has been eradicated.

Vaccination for foreign travel

When you are planning a trip abroad it is important to find out which, if any, injections are advised or required. Those who have already had the usual injections will need no more than a gamma globulin injection for most countries. Gamma globulin protects against epidemic jaundice, a widespread disease in the countries bordering the Mediterranean Sea. The injection must be given a few days before the journey and provides protection for 3–6 months. If the destination is further afield a more thorough course of inoculations will be necessary. Your doctor, or the local child-health clinic, will inform you about which vaccinations are compulsory and which are advisable.

Hyposensitization

Inoculation against allergens (substances which can cause allergies) is called hyposensitization. What happens is that the child is given gradually increasing doses of the allergen. So far, most success has been obtained with extracts of pollen and of bee and wasp venom.

Survey of vaccinations

Vaccinations	Time	Reaction	Duration of the protection
Diphtheria, pertussis,* tetanus	3 injections at 3, 5–6 and 9–11 months	the child can become a little feverish, loses some of his appetite; the site of the injection is usually sore	the diphtheria and tetanus vaccinations have to be repeated
Polio	3 doses of vaccine given by mouth at the same times as the diphtheria and tetanus vaccinations	none	the vaccination has to be repeated
Measles	1 injection at 14 or 15 months	a third of all children become slightly feverish and have a slight rash	it is still not known how good the protection is or how long it lasts
Diphtheria, tetanus	repetition at about 5 years of age	the site of the injection is usually painful	the tetanus vaccination has to be repeated at 15–19 years
Polio	repetition at about 5 years of age	none	the vaccination has to be repeated at 15–19 years
German measles	1 injection in girls between 10 and 14 years of age	the child can suffer from joint pains	still not known
Tuberculosis†	1 vaccination at about 13 years	the site of the vaccination may be sore and stiff	lifelong

*The whooping-cough vaccination can be omitted altogether, or given separately.
†Some parts of the country are offering the vaccination to all new-born babies.

Dental care

Sound teeth are much to be prized, for the sake of both health and appearance. By teaching a young child good eating habits and the care of his teeth you will spare him many dental problems in later life.

Brushing the teeth

Get the child used to brushing his teeth early in life; start him off at one year of age, when the first milk teeth are cut. You will have to check that he is brushing his teeth properly, until the child is eight or nine years old, but let him take an interest in it himself so that he builds up good habits.

The teeth should be brushed at least twice a day, in the morning after breakfast and in the evening after the last meal of the day. The toothbrush must be a soft one and should have a short head with dense bristles and a solid handle.

Visiting the dentist

Arrange for your child to have regular dental examinations from the age of three. Even milk teeth, which are cut before the permanent teeth, need professional attention, and if there is a cavity in one of them it has to be filled. If the milk teeth decay so badly that they have to be extracted the child can find chewing difficult, and his dental problems may later include crooked teeth.

What is caries?

When a child eats sweets between meals there is a strong possibility that he will get cavities in his teeth. When something is eaten that contains ordinary sugar the bacteria in the mouth which live on the surface of the teeth form acids capable of attacking the teeth. If these acids are regularly allowed to do their destructive work little holes will be made in the teeth, and this is known as caries.

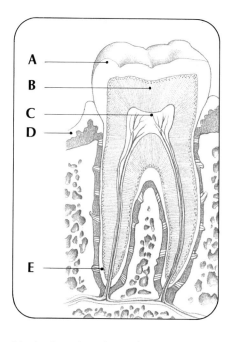

Vertical section of a tooth.

A. *enamel;* **B**. *dental bone;* **C**. *pulp;* **D**. *gum;* **E**. *root.*

Brush your teeth as shown

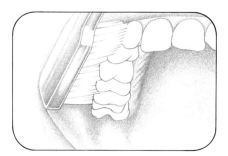

First brush the outsides of the upper teeth. Set the bristles at an angle against the edge of the gums and brush with small, short scouring movements.

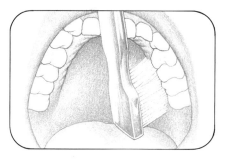

Next brush the insides of the upper teeth. Begin on the left behind the last molar. Feel if the brush is following the edge of the gum.

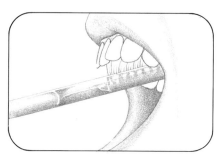

When brushing the backs of the upper teeth, hold the brush as shown. Use small, short strokes.

Fluoridization

Nowadays it is common knowledge how important it is for children to have a sufficient intake of fluoride, especially when the teeth are developing. Fluoride strengthens the enamel and makes it more acid-resistant. Fluorides occur naturally in drinking-water, but in quantities that vary from place to place. The health centre, clinic and the dentist will know details of the fluoride content in your local water-supply. If your water has too little fluoride in it the deficiency can be made good by fluoride tablets which are meant to be taken from the age of six months until the permanent teeth begin to come.

Straightening the teeth

It is quite usual for the teeth to be crooked – uneven development of the jaw will cause this – and they may have to be straightened. The best results are obtained when the fault is corrected during certain periods of growth. These periods vary from child to child. The ortho-dontist can determine the right time and the most suitable method of correction.

Damaged teeth

Go to the dentist immediately if your child's teeth have been injured. If a permanent tooth has been knocked out there is an excellent chance that it can be reset with good results. Make sure that you take the child to the dentist as quickly as possible, preferably within a couple of hours.

Because a tooth is very sensitive to drying out it must be kept in a clean, tightly sealed plastic bag during the trip to the dentist; this will preserve its moisture.

When a tooth has loosened but is still in the mouth, try to stop the child biting on it. Roll up a handkerchief and stick it between the other teeth, so that the child's mouth is held open. Even injured milk teeth should be examined by the dentist because the formation of the permanent teeth might be impaired.

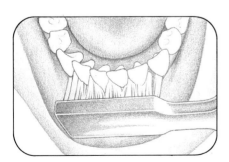

Now brush the outside of the lower teeth, one tooth at a time.

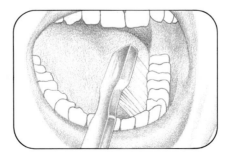

Brush the inside of the lower teeth, beginning on the left behind the last molar.

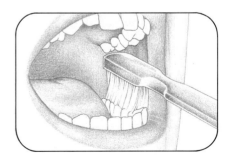

Finally, clean the grinding surfaces. Try to remove food particles from the cracks, as these are places where dental plaque (tartar) quickly forms.

Index